Making Sense of Toxic Abusive People

Dealing With, & Understanding Abuse & Bullying, Liars Toxic Personalities Partners & Narcissists, Manipulation & Gaslighting.
"Understand to Let Go & Find Peace"

Bringing Awareness to the Destructiveness of Bullshit, A Revealing Look at Bullshitter-Manipulator-Narcissist (BMN) Psychology and Behaviour, Leading to Self-Empowerment, Recovery, Peace-of-Being, and Social Consciousness Through Insight and Discernment.

Syl Sabastian
&
Elevia DeNobelia

Book One of: The Realism Series

"We first have to identify the depths of a problem before we can solve it."

"When we realise we can add to the World, change the World, contribute positively to the World, simply via being Aware, we undergo a profound moment of Personal Empowerment." - Biella Noble

"Wow awesome girl! Good for you! :) :)" - Ingrid Orosa

"Super Congratulations! I am so happy when I see someone accomplishing something full of purpose. Truly awesome." - Junel Doxie

"Bravo Syl. So true, bullshit is nothing but lies from those who have their own agenda. One can be easily fooled by a bullshit artist when they believe that everyone has some good in them. I suppose it's how I fell into my roomies trap of lies and bullshit. I want to believe everyone is a good person, but that simply is not so. :) :) :)" - Mary Berman

"Well done! I hope this gets into the hands of many, many people!!" -Tanya Jones Thibodeau Owner, Gateway Gazette, Entrepreneur, Author, Tech Teacher, Mom.

[On the Audio Book] - *"I appreciate your spoken word so much, I'm not able to describe with such eloquence. I have appreciated your verbal presentation of facts, partnered with real-life experience, and conscious appreciation of the human condition, to give clarity where there was none. Your ability to describe life's truth with heart-felt passion always keeps me listening."* - Sherry Ticktin

Special thanks to Michael Garrett, for editing and Andy Kefford (andykefford@gmail.com) for the cartoon jokes.

*

Contents

Ch0 - Empowerment - What's in it for you?

Hugo was determined to put an end to his Deja-Moo. His awareness sword glowed whenever he encountered bunk, malarkey, mumbo-jumbo, flubdub, fiddle-faddle, ackamarackus, tommyrot, crapspackle, blithery-poop, twaddle-cock, baldercrap, gentleman cow manure, and "truthiness".

Taking a Stand

"We have to take a stand against deception, take action against all lying, and together, as a society, using awareness, discernment, and understanding, empower ourselves to call bullshit against bullshit!"

Bullshit is a mind-virus, obscuring reality, disguising truth, and disconnecting us from sensibility, robbing us of our power and freedom.

What are we after, as individuals? We want to make sense of the world. We want to be able to deal with the world, not be victims, or be taken advantage of. Basically, we want to be able to see what's what, we want to know what's going on.

Why *don't* we have this? Because of bullshit.

Our awareness, our perceptions, our understandings, all too often are severely compromised by what's simply nonsense. Not only distortion pushed by individuals, but the falsehoods contained in convention. We grow up simply absorbing much that's rubbish, many mis-beliefs, faulty beliefs, cockeyed practises and standards which compromise us as individuals.

Mostly we're unaware of what we're unaware of. A difficult problem. Our aim is to draw attention to what affects us as individuals, via bullshit and bullshitters, using these as a mechanism, for not only spotting and understanding distortion, but for knowing ourselves.

Seeing bullshit, knowing bullshit, recognising bullshit, are powerful abilities which result from us developing that all-important trio of: **Awareness, Discernment, and Understanding**. Abilities vitally important for the war with deception we find ourselves in. A war in which our independence-of-being is at stake. If we can't spot the corruption, we don't even know we're being compromised, never mind how exactly. If we can't recognise bullshit, we can't recognise how we're being manipulated.

"Self-empowerment is fun!"

Self- Empowerment Through Understanding

Once we understand and are aware of bullshitter tricks, once we know their secrets, we disarm them of their power. Bullshit can't work on us once we're in the know, once we see the horseshit for what it is: deception, lies, and a hollow nothingness, all aimed at our manipulation.

This empowerment leads to fantastic benefits for the individual. We come to see not only the bullshit in society, in other individuals, but those bits of it inside ourselves, which affect us more than we typically realise. Those frustrations, those unknown annoyances and irritations, those botherations which afflict us without any obvious cause, these come from inner bullshit we're unaware of.

"Everything is suspect. A useful perspective. Treating bullshit as truth gets us into trouble, treating truth as bullshit, is caution, until we know better."

1

Much like computer viruses, which operate unseen, and make our computers perform poorly, so bullshit is a mental and emotional virus, affecting us in ways we don't always realise. This book is an anti-bullshit-virus program. Being aware of crapola leads to a clarity of being, to an exit from the fog of bullshit, a phenomenal difference of living and being. Empowerment via seeing through disguised deception is a powerful enhancement of our selves. An enhancement we wish to accomplish, through enabling the individual to see and know bullshit, which so sneakily affects us all if we're unaware.

Developing the tools of awareness, discernment, and understanding has a profound affect in all areas of our lives. Recognising and dealing with fuzzy crap, both external and inner, is but one major benefit. Understanding is the start. Without the ability to recognise bullshit, we're held back and restricted in our personal-development and self-improvement. We can't deal with what we don't see.

We dearly wish to see individuals empowered to deal with bullshit. Particularly in their immediate lives. Many suffer tremendously from devious deception, and don't have the tools for rectifying their situations. We're earnestly intent on empowering such individuals, and society in general. If most of us can change, learn, and grow in ways which allow us to recognise bullshit, and know awareness is a light, a light which banishes the shadows bullshit needs to survive, we can make a difference.

Bringing awareness, discernment, and understanding of bullshit into general consciousness will transform us as a society. If we look around at what's wrong, it's almost always indirect lying. The problem of untruth. This deception exists because as a society, as individuals, we're not always able to see nor recognise it fully. We know it's there, but don't know how exactly. We aim to change this lack of recognition, this lack of power. It's time to reclaim the sensibility which is our due, our due as aware, discerning, understanding, and empowered individuals.

"We can compromise on optional matters, like style. But how do we compromise on matters of ethics? We cannot. So there is compromise we can do, and compromise we can't. Seeing things for what they truly are, and not what we would like them to be, takes courage."

Ch1 - Why Bullshit is a Big Deal

Naturally made flora and vegetation growth and size enhancer. One-of-a-kind, limited supply. Fresh today. Get it while it's hot. Once in a lifetime deal.. today only..... priced to sell...

$99.99 a handful !!!

Nefarious Bullshit

"Bullshit is a cancer. At first, that initial little bit of cancer makes no difference, we don't even notice. Until later."

Bullshit has become a determining factor in the social media age, a defining issue of our time. Its influence is seen on the global stage. But bullshit is also local, where it presses us directly, where it's we ourselves who have to deal with this growing problem.

Not only is bullshit personal propaganda. Under the surface it's deception, manipulation, dominance, and gross negativity. It's no good to recognise this epidemic without being able to fully identify and understand all its nuance and subtlety. Especially with the bullshit we find in our day-to-day lives, as the manipulations and deceptions aren't readily obvious. Which really means we're being bullied by bullshit. Even worse, we allow this plague to flourish and grow because we don't adequately see all of what's going on. We get taken in, and, all too often, simply taken.

However, if we can recognise what the bullshitters are up to, understand all their tricks, and know their secrets, we can avoid their bad intentions. For they *do* have bad intentions. These aren't always easy to see. Another reason why bullshit is a serious issue, as it *IS* nefarious. Perhaps we've become lulled by the Hollywood implied notion it's basically harmless. But it's not, not even close.

We might think we're simply dealing with exaggeration or embellishment, thus no big deal, but this is a convenient avoidance of an unpleasant reality, allowing those perpetrating this blight on us to get away with their crap and to feel emboldened. No longer can we tolerate this nonsense. We but need to look around to see the severe consequences of bullshit which haven't been checked: politics, sexual harassment, fake news, trolls, advertising, bots, propaganda, social media, bullying, narcissism, opinion personalities, etc. etc.

All bullshit! The list is long, and why bullshit is a big deal.

"Be civilised. Civilisation is more than Law. Civilisation is standards, values, personal boundaries, respect, trust, and more. We need to be extra vigilant of the very beginnings of transgressions, in our homes, families, communities, society, in the world at large."

Close to Home!

Decent good people are taken in by apparently "friendly" deception, mainly because the idea someone could be so preposterous is simply not something they can readily believe. But bullshit *IS* preposterous. Bullshitters are very very preposterous. A key understanding vital for coming to terms with this particular form of distortion and lying.

As we shall show, there's a whole lot more to this falseness than we first realise. Bullshit is most intimately connected to manipulation, to ego, and its extreme version: narcissism. We will extend our focus to the bullshit-manipulator-narcissist, (The BMN) who are exaggerated versions of bullshitters. These individuals do much harm, in ways not always recognised. We aim to provide the tools for that recognition, and thus also the means for dealing with problematic abuse. If we don't step up our game, we become part of the problem, allowing the infection to fester and spread.

"Bullshitters are a mucking-fuddle, full of contradictions and square-circle logics, perpetually in a no-win game with themselves."

We have fantastic exemplifications of the bullshit-manipulator-narcissist constantly in the news. But these specific individuals aren't our focus. They serve as phenomenal examples, highlighting all we bring to light in this book. The danger lies mainly close to home. It's here we need to look in detail. As this corruption isn't as easy to spot when not under the magnifying glass of constant media attention. The damage and harm is no less great, actually greater, as it's closer, more personal, and pervasive. We wish to turn that illuminating lens on the beginnings of these monstrous personalities, allowing us to cut out this cancer on the world, right at the root.

The purpose of our book is to enable ordinary people, like you and me, to deal with the effects and consequences of bullshit and the bullshit-manipulator-narcissist in our every-day lives. We wish to enable recognition of deception with the people we know, with the people we have to interact and deal with. We aim to prevent the very real harm which interacting with phoneys and BMNs can cause, through being in the know, through personal empowerment.

"Once we know, we're empowered."

Dominance via Bullshit

Bullshit-manipulator-narcissists are focused on dominance, wanting to cheat and lie their way to superiority. They can only try to achieve their sad aim by attempting to pull others down "below" them. And this they do, causing significant harm. We're hugely thankful if this isn't something you've directly experienced. Sadly, we've seen it way too much, often manifesting as the bullshit-manipulator-narcissist obliterating another's self-worth with constant condescension, with persistent demeaning and derogatory denigrating behaviour, resulting in real harm, and hurt.

Horribly, this happens also with parents and their children, or with the elderly by their children in turn. Of course, manipulation and abuse is all too prevalent in the workforce, or any place power can be misused. Happening in any interaction and relationship, especially when there's some kind of dominance of one over the other. This behaviour is egregious, reprehensible, and unforgivable.

Generally, we're aware of typical bullying. Bullshit is also bullying, a subtle bullying, not so readily apparent, but no less harmful, and no less of a big deal. Our book aims to raise awareness about the very real negativity of bullshit, enabling us all to recognise what's happening. Allowing us to deal with previously unseen effects and consequences, thereby changing how we deal with bullshitters. Especially the bullshit-manipulator-narcissist.

"I shudder to think of the men, women, children, the elderly, who might not have the fortitude and self-assurance to deal with the kind of unrelenting negativity, and 'bonds of suffering' these bullshit-manipulator-narcissists perpetrate with their 'nice' and 'friendly' bullying bullshit. These are the folks who would benefit from understanding exactly what's being perpetrated, and this awareness of the motivations behind the hierarchical mindset of the BMN will empower them. An awareness which can set them free."

Bullshit is Lies

Our book has a serious tone, because it's a serious matter. There's something very wrong with society's perception of bullshit, and it needs to change. For instance, we looked up bullshit and lie at thesaurus.com. Bullshit has one section only, most unusual in how little there is. All its synonyms are benign and no big deal.

Under lie, there are nine pages of sections. As we'd expect, listing all the huge variety related to lying. But not once is bullshit listed as a synonym for lie! Not once! Why is that? This discrepancy is the serious deficiency in societal consciousness the book addresses. Most people don't make the connection that bullshit *IS* lying. But it *IS* deception, it *IS* dishonesty, plain and simple.

This distorted perception of lying enables bullshitters to get away with bullshit. They trade on this acceptance and excusing or softening of the corruption and seriousness of bullshit. We know how much it matters, but typically it's not seen as an actionable issue in society, despite its screwing everything up.

We tend not to think of bullshit as lies exactly, but it is. The difference is merely because lies are typically somewhat easy to prove or disprove. With bullshit it's difficult to say definitively, which is the appeal for the bullshitter. They can easily "get away with" what are really lies. Many lies, complex lies, disguised and concealed lies, implied lies, suggested lies, hinted lies, lies of impression and innuendo, lies of tone, mood, vibe, and all mother of other subtle lies. All lies nonetheless. No matter how they might be dressed up and hidden, still lies.

The *intent* and agenda behind those lies remains, and it's all to present an untruth, to conceal truth, to cover truth, to hide truth. The aim is to project and "sell" untruths as truths. That's lying. Just because it isn't clear, obvious, and overt doesn't make it any less a lie. In fact, there's the lie that it's not a lie, compounding the lying.

"The more they deny, the more they lie."

Bullshitters like the vagueness and undefined nature of bullshit, because then they can't easily be pinned down. Their personal propaganda, and they themselves, are thus a moving target, able to adapt and refine subsequent behaviour to deal with any "attacks" on credibility. All manner of "tricks" are used to evade being "caught out." Bullshit is used to defend, excuse, justify, rationalise, and otherwise prevent any attempts at exposure.

The Big Deal of Understanding

"The preferred solution to cancer lies in prevention."

A bullshitter's tricks and methods are many. The entire subject doesn't follow neatly from A to Z. Rather, all the component elements cross-connect with each other. To come to a full understanding is to also fully understand the psychology and motivations of the bullshitter.

Bullshit is a big deal, intimately connected to the manipulation it really is, and closely linked to ego, especially its extreme form: narcissism. These are the main motivating factors. Both ego-narcissism and manipulation have dishonesty as their core. Both attempt "getting something for nothing." Both are short-cut mindsets.

The intricacy of the relationships between bullshit, ego, and manipulations are complex, but we will lay out all the various aspects in detail throughout each chapter. To fully understand we need to glimpse the complexity from many angles. At first only seeing a partial view, and thus a full understanding won't yet be ours.

The individual chapters contain connecting overlap. In each chapter, when delving into the depths of that particular aspect of bullshit and the bullshitter, we use the other aspects of understanding, and as we go along, the connections and interactions become more and more obvious. Until it all leads to that *understanding* from which we simply know and recognise what's going on, without needing to remember any explanations.

Once we know the motives, the logics, the rationales, justifications, and substantiations of bullshit and the bullshitter, we'll simply know, and see right through their preposterousness.

Therefore, we deliberately repeat the various angles of understanding and key concepts relating to bullshit throughout the book allowing a thread to form, enabling a learning to take place which isn't dependent on remembering. We aim to come to a thorough *understanding,* for it's only when we understand the bullshitter from the inside that we're able to successfully spot the deceptions.

There's more to the entirety of bullshit, a knowing which will come through in the appropriate detailed insights of the various chapters. These chapters needn't be read in any particular order, except for the first and the last two.

"Complexity requires many looks, many perspectives, before the whole congeals into knowing."

The Bullshit of BS

We can see our differing attitudes toward this form of lying through how we use the terms BS and bullshit. BS is socially sanctioned, it's okay, acceptable, mild, non-offensive, no problem.

But bullshit is an ugly term, not used in polite society nor on mainstream TV. These different attitudes represent our general mindsets when it comes to bullshit. The benign version, and the ugly truth. We want bullshit to just be BS, but it isn't. Bullshit *IS* ugly. It's not only unpleasant, but harmful. Bullshit is nothing but lying. It may be lying in indirect ways, but it's still lying.

When we consider the intent behind bullshit, the matter is clarified. The intent is to deceive. There's no getting away from this disturbing reality. Deception is serious. So is bullshit. We can't be fooled by packaging. We can kid ourselves into trying to believe bullshit is just BS, but it's a big deal, a very big deal. Understanding and dealing with apparently benign lying for what it really is, matters. Matters a great deal, if we care about anything more than superficiality.

The more we okay bullshit, the more we end up living in a hollow, deceitful, unreal, crappy world. No thanks! There's much we CAN do when it comes to bullshit, and it's to this end our book is directed. The remedy lies close to home, seeing and dealing with the bullshit in our everyday lives. This is where we can make a profound difference.

"Why cancer and bullshit? Because both are insidious. Both unnoticeable initially as a threat, both slowly eating their way into our lives, both causing more and more harm. Both need to be stopped early on, before they take over, before it's too late."

Ch2 - Leveraging Preposterousness

Unbelievable Implications

"Preposterousness, and its inherent lunacy, is well-disguised by its very obviousness. We can become enablers when we refuse to believe someone would resort to such absurdity. We cannot comprehend nor do we wish to deal with the sheer ridiculousness and wrongness of it all. It just should not exist. Yet it does. We've played a part in its existence and continuing perpetration in our homes, families, and communities by refusing to acknowledge its implication."

Preposterousness is a tricky concept. The very idea of it is absurd. And that really is the problem. Our minds are simply boggled, usually preventing us from fully taking in all of preposterousness and its implications. It's especially the implications which are so troublesome. Good people find it hard to believe someone, anyone, who isn't an obvious raging lunatic confined to a madhouse can behave in ways which should put them there. It goes against every sensible, good, honest, and believable fibre of our being. Yet, this is exactly what happens.

Bullshitters use our reluctance to believe preposterousness to their advantage. They exploit the understanding that if they're going to lie, make it an outrageous lie, as it's hard to believe someone would actually do such a thing. Then it becomes a matter of *how* the lie is told. We get presented by a choice. Either we believe the lie, or we have to believe someone was utterly outrageous, utterly absurd, utterly ridiculous, and utterly preposterous in the telling of the lie.

"Top Definition: Fronting - Acting like you are more, or you have more, than what really exists."

We're in essence being asked to believe the person who told the lie, usually a normal enough appearing person, is in actuality someone capable of this madness. For most, this is difficult, even near impossible to conceive. When our logic conflicts with what we perceive, we tend to believe our perception. If the bullshitter *appears* reasonable and normal, we refuse to believe they're actually crazy. However, when we look at ridiculous behaviour, it really is crazy. This trick is helped by the fact that absurdity is usually just an occasional behaviour. At least, as far as we know. But, as we shall see, with the bullshitter and the bullshit-manipulator-narcissist, everything about them is preposterous.

When we're asked to choose between believing what's said or promised, and the person saying it, we have to pay attention. Bullshitters use this insidious trick to fool us. They know it's especially difficult to disprove a promise, and hard to prove a person is being ludicrous. Their bullshit skills help them leverage preposterousness in this way. They know we don't want to, and can't easily, believe their exaggerated excess, which really, when we look at it closely, is a massive manipulation and an outright wickedness.

Extreme Absurdity

"Preposterousness can't really be described, only understood. Preposterous people assume a stance, position, and attitude that's totally and absolutely unjustified, which prevents them from easily being questioned, called out, and closely scrutinised, because no sensible person would think someone would so falsely and inaccurately portray themselves to the length and measure which preposterous, seemingly 'nice,' bullshitters do."

The bullshitter's entire being, their entire facade, their entire constant performance is preposterous. They are preposterous people. Everything they do, because it's false, phoney, and staged, is absurd. Even more ridiculous are the motivations underlying such extreme behaviours.

It's hard to believe someone would go to such extreme lengths, that someone would devote their every action and behaviour to feed and maintain a lie, simply because of their ego, simply to satisfy their desperation for attention and approval. It's difficult to comprehend someone would forgo learning and growing as a person, and devote themselves to replacing realness with bullshit. Yet, it happens, it exists. We almost have to treat bullshitters as aliens, for in this, they're not in the least normal.

Ridiculous Under-Development

"The incredible insistence by the bullshit-manipulator-

narcissist on foisting their indulgence on others is developmentally arrested, even stopped. To just insist, insist, insist on indulgence... is unbelievable in its inappropriateness! This is nothing but psychological stalking!"

The bullshitter, as a person, is behind. Radically behind. The problem, for them, is knowing this, one of the reasons for their bullshit ways in the first place. They pretend to cover their lacking, which they became aware of, usually at a fairly young age.

From there, because they refused to accept they're not wonderful and fantastic, as they want to believe, and had believed, they resorted to pushing illusion to compensate for this undesirable reality. The ridiculousness of their solution aggravates the problem. Their vacuum-of-being just keeps getting emptier and emptier, until they're a preposterous husk, knowing only how to front their delusion.

Outrageous Arrogance

"Arrogance is easy! It requires little effort, no skill, and no substance! The easiest bullshit of all. Arrogance pushes entitlement, superiority, 'specialness,' subjugation, status, and position."

Bullshitters aren't always obviously and outwardly arrogant. Internally, almost inevitably so. They tend to believe they "should" have more, that they actually are more, and that they "deserve" more. Their arrogance is monumental. It's their arrogance, that unsupported belief in their value and capability, which drives and fuels their hype of self. The bullshitter's arrogance is utterly preposterous. Arrogance itself is preposterous, a particular form of bullshit, and as such, comes naturally to the bullshitter.

Particularly preposterous in the bullshitter, as there's
nothing at all to back it up. Their arrogance is typically
covert, but when they transition to overt arrogance, this is
a dangerous shift, as they will only do so if they feel
empowered. A look at any dictator will reveal evidence of
this.

However, our focus here is about the local bullshitter, the
local tyrant, the abusive spouse, caregiver, boss, or even
friend. In this, that brazen arrogance is a kind of gift for
us, as it makes these bullshitters easy to spot. We need to
remember easily recognised external arrogance is more of
an exception when it comes to the bullshitters we
encounter in our day-to-day. Paying attention to gross
examples and exaggerations helps significantly when it
comes to identifying the often more subtle instances of
these attitudes in the bullshitters of our everyday lives.

"Arrogance actually causes stupidity!"

Vital Frame-of-Perception

Preposterousness is the defining perspective which
frames everything about bullshit and everything which
follows in this book. Understanding that the bullshitter,
the BMN, everything they do, everything they are, and
how it all connects to the preposterous, is essential for
coming to terms with gross fronting. Understanding
bullshit needs to be preceded by perceiving the
ridiculousness and absurdity of it all. The deeper we go
into understanding, the more vital this frame-of-perception
becomes. Otherwise the mind just refuses to accept what
they do, as it's too crazy, and we assume there "must be"
some other explanation. We don't know what, but it can't
be what it seems, because that would be too preposterous.

When it's too absurd to believe, we fill in logical and reasonable explanations to rationalise unbelievableness. Once we understand this about ourselves, it becomes much easier to understand bullshit and the bullshitter. Keeping in mind this perspective of the craziness of it all, when it comes to the other aspects of bullshit discussed in this book, is extremely helpful. Overcoming "it's hard to believe" is the first step to recognising and dealing with bullshit.

"If we find ourselves defending the outrageous, making excuses for them, and looking at it 'from the other side,' we need to take care. It's then we're in danger of not believing what's too unpleasant to believe."

Ch3 - Deep-Seated Causality

"Don't even look his way Gladys. He thinks he saw himself on a 'Shark Week' documentary 8 years ago and he'll try to autograph your fin!"

Understanding

"The constant transgressing of their own conscience bothers the bullshit-manipulator's ego, causing shame and guilt, resulting in the perpetuation of bullshit upon bullshit."

Once we understand what drives and motivates someone, we understand them more easily. Also, full understanding releases us from stress. After all, we don't hold it against the lion for wanting to eat us, or become angry with the lion for wanting to do so. We don't like it, but we understand why. Knowing why allows us to take appropriate action.

Understanding is likewise a powerful tool for dealing with what's wrong, unethical, and detrimental. It removes the cloudiness and fog of over-emotionality, which usually causes us to aggravate the situation. Understanding is our way out.

This is especially so when dealing with the BMN. Their psychology is somewhat more complex and convoluted. We can come to know them and understand how they work inside through understanding their distortions. It's by their contortions they are defined.

The point is about the importance of understanding why something is done, whatever the reason. It's to take that same mechanism we use with the lion and applying it to the bullshitter, even though their actions aren't motivated in the same way. If we understand the motivations, we're able to deal with actions more appropriately when it comes to our emotions.

We still don't like it. In the case of bullshitters and BMNs especially, it's still wrong, manipulative, mean and nasty etc. But it doesn't throw us out, because we understand. We understand how they're caught up in an extremely idiotic and limited psychology, a bubble of ridiculousness. This allows us to not be confused, discombobulated, or have other disruptive states-of-mind which result from lack of understanding. We can deal with their crap more objectively, more sensibly. We don't lose our heads.

Understanding the bullshitter and the extreme version of the bullshit-manipulator-narcissist is extremely useful when it comes to identifying those small and often subtle aspects of bullshit within ourselves. When we have a gross exaggerated example to draw from, seeing the vague and nebulous inside ourselves is much easier. We learn about our hard-to-perceive inner hold-backs, from a good understanding of such psychological limitations in others, especially the glaring examples found in the bullshitter and BMN.

Conceit

"Privately, bullshit-manipulators insist the rules apply to everyone else, but not to them. A level playing field isn't desired. The king-be status is insisted on, and coerced, to manipulate a situation where their questionable behaviour and squirreliness isn't questioned - they want the benefits, without the detriments, to their persona and image."

The ego-conceit of the BMN is a core cause of their distorted psychology. The insistence on their "specialness," and thus how what applies to others, doesn't to them, is fundamental to understanding how they perpetrate what's grossly unfair in any definition of the word, even while insisting "fairness" be applied to themselves.

This complete separation of what applies to them, and what applies to others, is hard to comprehend unless observed. Somewhere along the line they picked up this peculiar *entitlement*. They see it as something which *makes* them special. This distorted belief is connected to their deep conviction that "putting one over others" is a deep *good* and is extremely desirable. If they can "put one over others," it "proves" their specialness. This gross mis-belief and its consequences shapes much of their psychology.

When we get into causality, starting at such levels, it all flows from there. The key is to realise when we look at it now, from our detached, reasonable, and logical perspective, those distorted beliefs are seen for what they are. At the time these beliefs were acquired by the bullshitters, there was no perspective, only belief, a certain trust, and acceptance. Mostly these beliefs aren't consciously acquired.

Later, typically, only the last few steps in the causality

chain are ever paid any attention. To go back all the way to the root is too scary a proposition for the bullshitter. At some time this was attempted, but the sheer gross f-ed-up-ness of their beliefs and consequential actions was way too much to handle. So that avenue is never pursued again. This refusal to deal with that deep messed-up-ness of the BMN is one of the additional reasons for their immersion into bullshit. Just one more reason.

"Conceit is a peculiar form of blindness."

Once we've established an identity-of-self, we generally acquire some measure of conceit. The very definition of our identity is us saying, "this is good." And so it is, usually. Unless we become locked to that identity, usually via conceit. If we can't upgrade our personal definition, if we're unable to adjust our view of ourselves, we move from self-appreciation to conceit. A conceit which typically limits adjustments to the self when it involves realisation of personal foolishness. Conceit won't allow us to acknowledge that our self is flawed or compromised in any significant way.

In our quest for personal empowerment, we can learn from the bullshitter. We can leave our personal definition open, leave space for adjustment and alteration, leave space for the acknowledgement of personal folly. Unless we're able to admit to our silliness as we become aware, as we discern, as we understand more about ourselves, we won't learn and grow; we'll become stuck in that conceited limiting view of ourselves.

Flexibility of self is a lesson conceit doesn't easily allow. Seeing the severe restrictions of conceit in the BMN is useful for understanding its limitations within ourselves, a limitation not always easy to perceive when looking inward.

Avoidance

"The top-dog, bottom-dog mindset and denial of limited awareness are serious impediments to the evolutionary mindset."

It's imperative to understand, with BMNs and with people in general, there's seldom a *single* cause to "explain" someone. We in vain persist in looking for such simplistic solutions when they don't exist. Even worse, we latch onto some singular simplistic explanation out of pure laziness. Our own bullshit which can lead to severe distortions.

"Bullshit-manipulator-narcissists at root know they're utterly crappy and all their preposterous, ludicrous, and ridiculous actions, seen and unseen, are about avoiding the ugliness of who and what they really are."

The causality of this avoidance is aggravated by a sudden awareness or awakening at some point. At that moment, they looked back at themselves with awareness, realising just how utterly *foolish* and dumb they've been, typically realising how *they* have been conned and used in some way. How someone has "put one over" *them*. Usually this will be a parent or some other influential person in their young lives who was a bullshitter, and they came to realise and be aware of the full extent of that bullshit.

Since by the time this awareness or awakening occurs they're already deeply immersed in the superiority, ego, vanity, "looking good" and not ever "looking bad" paradigm, this awareness of just how absurdly foolish, naïve, ignorant, stupidly trusting, and idiotic they were for believing bullshit, is a mightily painful blow.

One they never forget, and never forgive. An experience

they'll do everything to erase. Thus the bullshit begins. Especially the inner bullshit to cover this awareness that they're not nearly as smart, clever, aware, and otherwise as fantastic as they've believed, and would like to believe.

That hype of self is usually put on them in some way by another, and they swallowed it completely. Likely as a mollification of the awful truth. Just how do you tell a kid they don't live up to even your most modest expectations? If the guidance in their lives came from those locked to ambition, success, and superiority, they likely had bestowed high hopes on the young future bullshitter, and the resulting disappointment when that bubble burst was covered by even further hype, praise, and other ego stroking. But that underlying disappointment can't easily be disguised.

Inevitably, this understanding of their lack of wonderfulness is realised by the bullshitter, one of the causes of their bullshit psychology. They need to cover this truth at all costs. The resulting negativity from that personal awareness is hugely influential, both in terms of leading to "proving" how wrong this perception and truth of them is, and in covering up that truth and the resultant pain. Typically they will cling to that initial expectation and hope of "greatness" from them. The strong positive emotional associations from that period in their lives, when they were held in such high esteem, is a comfort they don't want to forego.

That over-estimation and hype of them they use as their personal self-definition, and as subsequent justification for all their one-sidedness. When a psychology has been convinced at a very young age they're the most wonderful person in the entire world, that they're phenomenally special, it can lead to severe distortions of being. Especially if the reality of what they are turns out to be very far from this distorted over-expectation.

"For the bullshitter, indulgence trumps everything."

Making peace with our own nincompoopery is a vital skill, essential for self-growth and awareness. The more we discern, the more we understand, the more we realise what in the past seemed good is no longer so. We can't avoid this truth. It's not a problem unless we avoid adjusting. That adjusting involves acknowledgement, internally, of some form of lack-of-awareness. It's not a big deal if we look at it this way.

How will we become more aware if it doesn't involve understanding of our unawareness in some way? It's a reality we can't avoid, not if we're honest, not if we wish to develop as individuals. Avoidance of this reality has dire consequences, severe limitations easily seen in the bullshitter.

Narcissism

"Bullshit-manipulators cross the line into delusion; wanting to believe, and believing, they can do whatever they want. This embolsters the underlying narcissist psychology. Crossing one unscrupulous line emboldens stepping over other ethical lines."

The slippery slope of bad behaviour leading to more, combined with narcissistic indulging, keeps leading bullshitters astray. Their chosen delusions are important to them. Extremely important. Those delusions sustain them, motivate them, and provide their life focus. It's a mess, as they're perpetually chasing a nothing.

The piling on of self-aggrandisement on top of self-aggrandisement leads to the narcissism. They have to in the end believe they're the most wonderful thing ever, otherwise the entire precarious edifice collapses. No wonder when anything at all occurs which disproves this belief in any way, it leads to intense anger and stress, along with ridiculous efforts to counteract the threat.

"Understanding bullshit-manipulation is about understanding preposterous mindsets, attitudes, ethics, personal greed, self-critique-avoidance, and the inability to face awful-self-truths. This lack of sensibility is colossal, absurd, and outrageous, thriving on chaos."

At issue here is the internal reality and perceptions of the BMN. Their own "knowing." A contradictory affair, ranging from narcissism to self-loathing, all existing simultaneously. They utterly believe, for instance, they're crap as people, with good reason, but just because they have been and are now crap doesn't, of course, mean there's no hope for them. They believe this in their subjective perspective, and sadly, making it a self-fulfilling truth. Indeed, objectively, there *IS* some good in them, as one of the distinguishing characteristics of the bullshitter is their obsession with squaring their conscience. The fact they even attempt this means there's some good in them.

Unfortunately, they resort to bullshit, fudging, squirming, distorting, and other squirreliness to appease their consciences and boost their over-demanding egos. Their resort to bullshit in an attempt at squaring matters is what distinguishes them from out-and-out criminals. A label they assiduously make every effort to avoid. They do decidedly want the benefits of criminal behaviours, but without the smudge on their ego.

"Excessive vanity and self-importance sometimes compensates for lack of self-acceptance, in an attempt to obfuscate unpleasant awareness of awful self-truths."

Certainly there's an acute internal awareness of this belief of theirs that they're crappy. A reality their narcissism utterly and absolutely refuses to face, deal with, or acknowledge. Any negativity of self pops the bubble-of-specialness, and therefore they're no longer something which has value, and thus "needs" to be unhappy. It's an all-or-nothing psychology, hence the incessant need for bullshit, because, like the rest of us, they're not perfect. They acknowledge this also. But, internally, they have a plethora of excuses and reasons as to why they're not. Not one of those reasons will have anything to do with them. All will be because of others, circumstances, bad luck, and such like.

Sadly, they just can't understand one can be imperfect and be happy. They don't understand personal happiness can come from sources other than praise, admiration, attention, and approval. This is a truly tragic fact of their existence. So preoccupied are they with their incessant ego demands that alternatives, even when patently obvious and immediate in their day-to-day lives, are simply not seen nor recognised. The blindness caused by ego-dominance is astounding, something all of us can take as a dire warning on the dangers of inappropriate immersion. Especially immersion into ego.

"Important differences exist between self-love, self-care, and self-kindness. Self-love can be narcissistic, self-care can be vanity, and self-kindness can be selfishness. Discernment is the potent application of awareness."

The narcissism of the BMN is a gross distortion hard to miss. Where does narcissism start? How does self-belief become narcissism, how is this possible? Through unchecked accumulation. Each little bit of added over-hype and over-estimation of self, each additional self-aggrandisement, in themselves small and relatively insignificant, add to this accumulated distortion of self-perception.

What do we take away from this understanding? How do

we prevent such a calamity in ourselves? By adding humility and modesty to what's important to us. By realising reality checks are necessary, and by fully understanding the myth of ego and the belief in the necessity of specialness to be happy. We but need look around to see plenty of regular folk who are plenty happy; way happier than any narcissist.

We can take heed from their bullshit mis-beliefs and look inside at what we subscribe to. Often those beliefs, such as the belief in "specialness," aren't particularly obvious. If we take these exaggerations and extreme distortions, and work backwards, looking at their origins, we come to see what perhaps lurks within. Perhaps for us, "specialness" masquerades as self-pity, or being a victim, or we overemphasise a particular talent. We only need to ask ourselves, as a self-check, "Is my belief bullshit? Am I distorting truth?"

"Insisting on self-honesty makes narcissism impossible."

Agendas and Beliefs

"Corrupt agendas and motivations lead to distorted perspectives, to inappropriate perceptions and behaviours. Lacking independence-of-being easily makes one inadvertently complicit via default unawareness and opens otherwise good people to manipulation and abuse."

Much as the bullshitter is governed by their distorted agendas and goals, we, too, have to pay attention to our own inner state. We may only have a fraction of this corruption, but, for the bullshitter, that little is enough. Their intimate acquaintance with their own distortions and bullshit makes them hyper-aware of the same in others. The difference is, in good people, that bit of bullshit is a shame, and something good people aren't proud of and certainly don't want exposed. They will deal with their own failings by themselves. To the BMN in particular, this is a gaping doorway to manipulation and exploitation.

We thus have to look at our own deep-seated beliefs which are the causality of our own behaviours. If we pay attention, we will see we hold some beliefs which lead to motivations we can't really justify. A deep personal matter, something that's part of being human, and the constant learning and growing which is life.

"None so easy to deceive as those so desperately willing to believe."

Its relevance here is that these personal flaws, and

especially if they're indulgences, when we knowingly engage in what *we personally* believe isn't good or wrong, these personal transgressions against ourselves make a huge difference when dealing with bullshitters and BMNs. They will actively look for these flaws in us and look to exploit them. We have to be extra vigilant of ourselves and our motives and beliefs when dealing with bullshit.

We simply need to look at people misled by bullshit promises. Inevitably it's their desperation for that promise to be fulfilled which causes them to swallow the bullshit. Why? Because they don't want to deal with their own inner distorted reasons for wanting this short-cut. They don't want to make the effort to learn, to investigate, to research, to check.

Or, they want something which isn't easily justifiable, like a racist motive or personal greed. Their own deep-seated mis-beliefs make them vulnerable to bullshit and to being misled and exploited. They're thus led astray by their own narcissism and false beliefs.

"Achieving a bullshit goal cannot result in satisfaction. Attaining a flawed ambition only ends in loss of hope."

Our own beliefs and agendas are often subtly influenced and affected without any action by ourselves. Paying attention to convention soon reveals what we simply assume to be valid, what we've adopted just because it's commonly believed, not because we ourselves specifically and deliberately believe what we've assimilated. All too often, unfortunately, the agendas of convention are bullshit; a bullshit we don't always spot unless we purposely look with awareness and understanding.

Bullshitters are handy for identifying these bullshit beliefs, especially those of convention, as they're attuned to what's popular and to what they believe most people value, adopting these beliefs and ambitions as a means to obtain approval. Typically exaggerating such assumed ideas. Useful for us when it comes to identifying this particular and subtle form of bullshit.

Emptiness

"Without heart, without genuineness, the dance-of-life is devoid of ecstasy and is reduced to chaotic sloppiness and indulgence."

Once we become aware of this void in the bullshitter, it becomes much easier to understand them. The bullshit is used initially to try to cover up this vacuum, or to fill it, but this cannot ever be. One can't fill nothing with more nothing. They somehow fail to realise their bullshit is nothing but nothing.

We also have to know and realise something else when it comes to that nothingness. It causes them to hate genuineness, happiness, goodness, and any positivity and realness-of-being in others. They hate true niceness and will try to destroy it, because, *by comparison,* it exposes them and makes them "look bad," actually "proving" their emptiness. Goodness thus reveals their badness, for they *DO* engage in many bad behaviours. Their anti-goodness to disguise faults is a deep and root cause of much of their behaviour.

Knowing this helps our understanding of them tremendously. Especially when it comes to their completely self-defeating, illogical, and irrational behaviours such as pulling down and trying to destroy the goodness of others. Others who are actually being nice and good to them. But so deep is their inner aversion to their own emptiness, and so convinced are they that they "must" be "better" than others, that they engage in these absurd self-defeating behaviours by distorting their perceptions when it comes to good and nice people. And all because of a severe mis-belief. The mis-belief of relative "superiority."

"Without earnestness and sincerity we're pathetic fools blown about by every fad and fancy."

Whenever we feel put-out, disgruntled, disturbed, or bothered for no particular reason, inner emptiness of some kind is often the cause. We can't be happy as a result of an un-reality or a mistaken belief, or because of bullshit of some kind. When we feel this way, it's a good time to re-examine what we've come to believe and adopt.

We don't always acquire these compromises consciously. Making that effort to come to awareness and discern our not-so-obvious beliefs is well worth the energy. The emptiness of the bullshitter serves as good motivation and insight.

Insecurity

"The root of the us-against-you mind-suck is to legitimise an indefensible personal illusion. It's dishonest. This is an unethical endeavour to make what's inappropriate and indulgent, legitimate. All because of the unrelenting insistence on indulgence."

Bullshitters, as a whole, might appear to be confident, outgoing, brash, or extroverted, but in actuality they're deeply insecure. Their insecurity permeates everything they do, everything they are. It's that very emptiness, or incompetence, or other shortcoming, many of them only in the perception of the bullshitter, which they're attempting to cover up and compensate for with their bullshit.

This deep insecurity causes them to easily feel "put upon" by those with strong characters, especially if those characters are independent of influence and convention. Standalone people are a significant threat to the bullshitter, because they have no pressure points. They can't be leveraged or manipulated, and they also see through the bullshit and feel free to say so.

"Those who lack self-acceptance tend to be adversarial. Sadly."

Those with independence-of-being are a severe threat to the bullshitter. When they encounter such people, they will do everything they can to try to pull them down and in some way "prove" they're "actually" full of it, just like the bullshitter.

They hate the fact that together-people ARE actually what they try to bullshit others into thinking they themselves are. But what particularly bothers them is the realness and genuineness of these people utterly destroys one of their chief excuses, the excuse of, "but everybody does it." No, everybody does *NOT* do it.

Insecurity-of-self is a simple fact of life. One honest people come to terms with because they've nothing to hide. If we're humble, we know we don't know everything, we know always having the solution immediately is unrealistic, we know these obvious truths.. And so what? Honest people simply know this as a fact and no big deal, unless we've adopted some measure of internal bullshit making insecurity an issue. This could be the bullshit of trying to be perfect, or of trying to do a best which is unrealistic.

Good people have to be careful when it comes to inappropriate-application-of-goodness. A subtle problem which can lead to inadvertent problems such as unwarranted insecurity. Together-people have made peace with that fact of personal insecurity. They've learned to trust their ability to learn, an option always open to those with patience, earnestness and humility.

Justification

"Weak foundation - weak character - suspect motivations - suspect agendas."

Another major part of their excuse and justification for being a bullshitter is that actually being what they pretend to be is "impossible." A myth they cling to with everything they have, because, for them, this myth justifies the necessity of their bullshit, or at least validates it in some way. Together-people with independence-of-being disprove this myth with their very existence, an existence the bullshitter resents, as it conclusively "shows them up" and disproves their convenient self-myth.

A problem for the bullshitter is that independent people who have their shit together aren't intimidated nor fooled by the bullshitter. The bullshit arguments, obfuscations, and all the other "tricks" of the bullshitter don't work on these individuals, leaving the bullshitter feeling "defeated." Of course this is their internal perception only. It has nothing to do with the together-individual. They typically don't care a fig about such nonsense. They don't subscribe to hierarchies and comparisons.

"The unrelenting insistence on indulgence corrupts unrelentingly."

For the bullshitter, hierarchy and comparison is their entire world. They will feel like a "loser" compared to independent individuals. They will see themselves as "less than," generally feeling utterly miserable via comparison. All through the doings of their ridiculous comparison-mindset and their preposterous egos. This leads to a particular remedy the bullshitter tries to employ to rectify this unhappy state for them. If only they knew how unnecessary it all is. But they don't, so what they do is enlist allies. At every opportunity they will try to engineer "us vs you" situations, against individuals they cannot bullshit or bully.

For instance, if the independent individual is in a conversation with someone, and that third person disagrees or questions, or displays even the faintest opening of possibility of "attack," the bullshitter will jump in and immediately "take sides," amping up whatever difference there might be, trying to make it into something.

Their hope of course is to get the third party to fight their "battle" for them. It doesn't matter that there was no animosity or competitiveness from the perspective of the independent individual. They don't care about the nonsense going on inside the bullshitter. All their misery from relative rankings and negative comparisons are all utter folly to the independent self. The bullshitter is unaware of all this, their consuming comparisons distorting their sensibility and blinding them to reality.

"Once you know one fool, other fools are revealed."

The bullshitter is so caught up in these mis-beliefs and delusions of self that "getting even" and "putting them in their place" becomes a very big deal to the bullshitter. When they get the slightest opportunity, they will try to instigate some kind of antagonism from others against the together-person in the hope they will get their "come-uppance."

This tactic of the bullshitter is a nasty, rotten, and disgusting behaviour, but one we need to be aware of, as it can lead to real trouble, especially when it comes to BMNs. They're so consumed by their narcissism they will go to extreme lengths to try to rectify this severe imbalance between them and the genuine person. The real and obvious differences, so unfavourable to the bullshitter, burns them, gnaws at them, and eats away at their ego incessantly. They can become obsessed with trying to get even, and pull down, those they deem "superior."

"The root of the us-against-you manipulation, is the vain hope the unsubstantiated and illusory will somehow automatically and magically be condoned and contorted into the valid, through the assistance of another. The root of the us-against-you mindset is lack of courage, character, and integrity. It's a looking for alliance and an attempt to bolster an indefensible indulgence and stance."

We need to exercise caution when it comes to exposing a bullshitter. Usually, just revealing a warning awareness we know what they're up to is enough. Especially if we do so without actually forcing the issue, allowing the bullshitter to "save face." Loss of "face" burns them deeply. When they're unable to bullshit their way out, they become excessively nasty and vindictive. Being "caught out" definitively is a consequence they absolutely cannot live with. The exposure of the deep truth about them is one of their most feared fears.

"Discernment is key. Discernment involves going past the mere perception of our underlying substantiations and making nuanced observations, especially with regard to that which is often overlooked or obfuscated."

Our personal justifications, substantiations, and validations can be tricky. We aren't always fully aware of them, often just assuming what we use to support our behaviour is true. Laziness or lack of time and effort are a factor. Mostly though, for good people, it's simply assumption.

We believe much which is purported to be true, and is in fact so. We take it for granted most others are honest also. Sadly, this gets us into trouble, typically leading to believing what, on the surface, seems sensible, but when we make the effort to look under the hood, we find the support a fiction and bullshit.

An awareness of how bullshitters use this assumption, that what's pushed as a truth has valid backing, is used to fool us, is useful when it comes to examining what lies behind our own beliefs and assumptions. It's especially with substantiations and validations where discernment is so critically important. If we're living according to what's hollow, that's a problem. Good people often do this inadvertently, simply because their goodness predisposes them to believe without checking.

But, our awareness and understanding of bullshit changes that. We come to know we have to check for ourselves, our beliefs have to come from our own efforts, efforts which include checking, validating, and substantiating. Only by doing this can we justify a full honest backing and support of what we've taken to be our own, of what comprises our sacred honest self.

Conformism

"The driving force behind the skewed action of manipulated condonance is the lack of independent thinking, and an aversion to standing alone and standing up for one's own principles, values, and truths, a consequence of subscribing to the pressures of conformity without discernment."

So attuned is the bullshitter to what's "cool" and what others believe will "look good" they don't realise how utterly dependent they are on the opinions and beliefs of others. Their entire focus and being becomes slaved to what others think, robbing them of independent thought. Bullshitters are so bent on controlling and dominating, on being superior, this contradiction of their psychology escapes them. They have to be focused on what others like and want, what they think, not only to supply others with what will impress them, but also to gain that much needed drug of approval.

The bullshitter, who so craves to be special and wonderful, becomes addicted to what others think. They're peculiarly dependent on those they seek to impress and those who criticise them. Bullshitters become dependent conformists, seeking through others the condoning of their behaviour, in the process surrendering whatever little bit of freedom they might have. The price they pay for the imagined benefits is way more than they ever bargained for, and when it comes to this "deal," they're stupendous "losers." Ironically, in their quest to be "winners," their own actions turn them into monumental "losers."

"Being social is sometimes a trap of a different kind, especially for the child-teenager. Often fraught with peer pressure, inadvertent assimilation, choices of being, and other subtle potential pitfalls."

Observing the bullshitter's connection to conformity can alert us to our own possible unintended adoptions, which we perhaps didn't choose. Conformity is a peculiar beast. It's not necessarily bad, but it's not particularly good either. When it comes to conformity, we certainly cannot just "go with the flow." Society, as a whole, is "more or less," sensible. That less, holds many potential dangers.

Simply conforming for conforming's sake will rob us of our precious individuality, leaving us feeling hollow and empty, without really understanding the cause. If, inside, we're not living according to what we've chosen for ourselves, freely, then it's no wonder we don't really feel.

How can we, if what we are isn't fully our own? The bullshitter's lack of independence-of-being, and their resulting hollowness, are a stark warning of the dangers of allowing outside forces to shape us. We pay a stiff penalty for not caring about that most precious of all possessions, our real self. Inner attention to what isn't truly ours, and choosing that which is, makes an inordinate difference to our realness.

Power Lust

"A scorpion asks a frog to carry it across a river. The frog hesitates, afraid of being stung, but the scorpion argues if it did so, they would both drown. Considering this, the frog agrees, but midway across the river, the scorpion does indeed sting the frog. 'But why?!' cries the frog. 'Because it's my nature,' the scorpion replies, as they both drown."

Why is it petty tyrants are so insistent on power? Why bother, why make all the effort, why take all the risks? It's precisely because their *entire* life and way-of-being is at constant risk of exposure. As over-promoting lying frauds, they risk exposure at every turn. This is their big fear. They're thus monumentally insecure. All the power-grabbing and acting tough is to appease this monumental insecurity. They try to get to that point, where even if they should be exposed, it wouldn't matter, because they will have the power to say, "So what?"

This is their fantasy anyway. All that happens if they do actually succeed in this power consolidation is their insecurity of exposure is simply replaced by physical insecurity. The threat of being removed from their perch, or worse, and thus typically paranoia, is the end result.

Their entire psychology is predicated on insecurity, because of course, the entire psychology, person, and personal history is built on lies and falsehoods. It's amazing how such absurd and preposterous behaviour all boils down to one simple issue. In this case, insecurity.

"Desperation finds desperation."

What price do we pay for our desperations? Likely this isn't a question we'll ask, nor will it be appropriate for most people. We can see the answer in the bullshitter. How does this relate to us? We can look at any drive or desire which we have and ask if the effort is worth the reward. All too often it's not, all too often we pursue goals only because of the mistaken belief we "should."

If there's anything which corrupts us way more than it should, it's "should," which holds a peculiar power. We needn't be enslaved by this most tricky of subtle bullshits if we maintain a constant alertness and vigil. Our remedy is to constantly ask why. Both from ourselves and the world at large, the answer to why isn't always what we imagine. Often, there's no reason at all, but simply the just because, of "should."

Not good enough by far.

"We shouldn't should on ourselves."

Self-Deception

"Bullshitters are peculiar conformists. They subscribe to 'should' because this they believe is what others want to see and hear, and what will get them approval and attention."

It all boils down to the simple accumulation of lies. Their self-lies. How great they are, how wonderful, how deserving, how competent, how important, etc. etc. All the ego-lies. Their self-lies are also the lies they tell others. So they create these lies about themselves, and sometimes they inadvertently reveal their lies, then their insecurity just escalates. So this makes them escalate the bullshit and lies to cover up, and on and on it snowballs. For this mindset, they don't want to face the awful truth, like most do, and deal with it, and change. Oh no, they refuse. So they can't stop, they carry on, trying to cover it all up. Hence their massive insecurity and incredible self-deception.

Bullshitters are all bluster and "go," a self-important show. A fake. Nothing is really real, merely a self-created phoney persona resulting from immersion in the superiority paradigm. A perfect pawn. Those who manipulate are also easily manoeuvred.

Superiority complexes are born out of inferiority complexes. Money, status, and position don't buy confidence. It just makes for a bigger bully. These never truly satisfy their base insecurity, a big problem. Your basic home-grown chip on the shoulder looking to validate itself. But only integrity can do that, not bullshit and lies.

"The lack of ability and/or desire to think past the immediate and obvious surface perception is integral to the externally-influenced-persona. The externally-influenced-persona isn't the original content creator of themselves, their character, their personality, and their self-worth."

Once we learn to self-deceive, what a web of lies we weave. Such penalties await those who fall into this trap. Much like our physical body can become out of sorts by the smallest influence, so too the inner self is finely balanced. Each distortion in the internal world needs to use energy from somewhere else to maintain the balance. Energy which is much better used elsewhere, energy which is now unproductive.

Even worse, these distortions have a trickle-down effect, disrupting our system in unforeseen ways. If ever we've messed with a computer's system and seen what trouble even small, seemingly insignificant changes can cause, let this be a warning. Inner self-deception has the same effect. We always pay a price, but aren't always able to notice the effect directly. Always, these choices trade-off some perceived short-term benefit for a long-term detriment. A trade-off which compromises our integrity. Much like a ship, whose hull integrity has been compromised, disregard for the sanctity of our inner integrity leads to a slow sinking.

Origins

"Understanding is recognising."

We must be careful in assuming the high-profile examples of bullshitter-manipulator-narcissists, which we see so intimately in today's ever-present media, don't fool us into thinking this psychology is only found among the power-hungry and super-greedy. It isn't only found in places of power and wealth. The sad truth is this persona can be found everywhere, at every "level" of society.

We simply need to remind ourselves the "famous" examples started in someone's family, as someone's neighbour and friend. Bullshitters only become more noticeable as their confidence grows, but the underlying psychology remains the same, no matter how muted it may be in the beginning stages. One of their deepest drives is to attain some sort of external validation. Once they believe they've attained this "proof", their narcissism takes over, now validated, and the compounding shitball of their preposterousness is unleashed.

Paying attention to how the underlying causality of bullshitters, manipulators, and narcissists starts in those we know in our everyday lives and how those famous examples are simply exaggerations of what we encounter is most helpful when it comes to recognising these individuals before they become extreme.

"Bullshit destroys lives!"

Our most earnest intent with this book, is to make sure you, our reader, you personally, don't suffer needlessly as a result of a bullshitter or a bullshit-manipulator narcissist in your personal life. We dearly wish you find some assistance here when it comes to empowering yourself to recognise and deal with bullshit.

We see the resolution to the problems of the world, starting with you, the individual, at that personal and local level. If we each, in our small way, develop that discernment which leads to the awareness and understanding of bullshit, we prevent this corruption on the world from spreading and growing, weeding it out at the source, and improving the lives of good persons like yourself in the process.

Ch4 - All About Appearance

Image

"Being human isn't a forgone conclusion... we have to become... When we look beyond the con of the facade, we see a vibe, tone, energy foisted on us, and a rather preposterous caricature is perceived."

Their appearance, how they "look" to others, their image, how others perceive them, this is of the utmost critical importance to the bullshit-manipulator-narcissist. (BMN) What they show to the world is a facade, an unreality, a pretence, a sham. Their attempted portrayal of themselves is false, a fiction, a distortion, a non-reality they use to cover the not-so-good reality of what they really are. They're perpetually fronting. This false representation is a short-cut, a cheat to reap the benefits of others thinking and believing they're something they aren't. Thus, the bullshitter is always presenting themselves as more than the truth of themselves. And when interacting, we will inevitably get *less* than promised from them.

What's the difference between how regular people and bullshitters deal with their image? Honesty. It's as simple as that. Once we become aware of ourselves, aware of the concept of image, it's hard to be unaware of it. But genuine people don't lie about their image. They don't try to present a false image. In our ongoing quest for self-improvement, if we keep this in mind and pay attention any time we're tempted to fudge anything concerning our image, we would do well to remember the bullshitters and pay attention to what's happened to them, where they've ended up, and to their foolish empty lives, all because of those little fudgings. When it comes to bullshit in these matters, a little is a lot.

Pattern

"Paying attention to pattern reveals many secrets."

Good, sensible, normal people have trouble imagining or believing someone could be so entirely false and phony, so entirely made up, staged, and geared so exclusively to presenting a self which isn't real. One of the mechanisms the BMN uses toward this end is co-opting the latest trends of being, or personality key aspects and buzzwords. There's typically some popular focus which they leverage and use to "blend" and appear not only normal, but cool, hip, with it, and in some way "better" or special.

Over-usage of these fashionable terms, and making undue effort to portray their usage, is one way to identify the BMN. Particularly if we pay attention over longer time periods. They will be seen to shift with the tide of what's fashionable and "cool." The bullshitter is easily recognised by their incessant self-promotion.

What are our patterns? What do they say about us? How can we learn from them? A useful tool for self-understanding.

Pretence and Vanity

"A new version of bullshit is the bullshit of not appearing as a bullshitter."

Bullshit has entered a new phase in the internet and social media age, as people wise up, are alerted and warned by their friends. The BMN now has to join the crowd in pretending to be anti what they practise. Indeed, their voices will be the loudest, they always tend to overdo, they can't help themselves. They always have to stand out and be seen to stand out. Their need for attention is a powerful addiction which perverts their entire being, and with it their sense of balance and propriety. They can without qualm pretend to be strongly against exactly what they actually are.

"Vanity is bullshit. By being vain, you declare yourself a bullshitter."

By vanity we mean excessive and obsessive interest in superficial appearance and the perceptions of others in this regard. The BMN's psychology is intricately linked to their physical appearance. They're so obsessed with the overall image they push, that each part, integral to the whole, is manicured with the utmost attention.

"Appearance is a strategic focus, not a necessity."

Their "look," both literally and figuratively, is of

the utmost importance to them. So important it's *never* out of their awareness. They will be constantly primping, checking, and fiddling with their appearance. A hyper-awareness of their tone and attitude pervades what they do. If they're intent on projecting a certain image and appearance, they can be remarkably controlled, suppressing their natural inclination to an astonishing degree. Sadly, they can "behave" nicely and sensibly only when motivated by some idea of benefit. Behaving nicely simply for the sake of niceness unfortunately isn't part of their logic.

"Vanity makes you ugly."

Sadly, this the BMN doesn't realise. Their obsession makes them unappealing. Once observed, we see the utter unreality, hollowness, and shallowness of who they are. Not just shallow, but callow. There's a coarseness to their inner being, a primitive pressure which reveals a complete lack of depth, and of what constitutes normal humanity. A sad business indeed, to observe how a person can be so thoroughly subverted by so facile a life-purpose.

How much is the issue. How much are we concerned with our appearance, how much vanity? It's difficult to gauge, but when we look at the BMN, and narcissists in general, it's easy to see what's too much. We need to control our appearance, not have our image control us.

Counter-Cool

"To the externally-influenced-persona, the quality of the input of others is determined by the perception of their image."

Since their image and appearance are entirely

determined by the perceptions of others, and since for the BMN this is so vitally paramount, they're as a consequence extremely influenced from outside. They tend thus to be amazingly conventional, even though they will deny this and would dislike the idea if presented to them. Nonetheless, it's true.

They like to think of themselves as "cool" and "special," as "ahead of the game," but in actuality, they're nothing of the sort, merely imitators. Aping whatever they can to get some sort of "shine" or advantage. True creativity and innovation isn't only too much effort, not a short-cut, and thus has no appeal, but is also way too risky. They could flop or fail, and heaven forbid they should be associated with such a calamity.

"Be careful what you pretend to be. You are what you pretend to be." - Kurt Vonnegut

Further, their perceptions of others are critically affected by appearance and image. They will radically upgrade the value of what a person says, or does, simply based on how "cool" they believe them to be.

Likewise, they will totally disregard someone they perceive as "uncool." Often being rude and dismissive of those they deem such, much to their own detriment. Their sensibility when it comes to interactions is severely compromised by this method of evaluation. It's also one of the principal mechanisms by which they gauge their own "value." One of the many reasons for their perpetual insecurity, as outside validations relying on appearance and cool, are typically fleeting and temporary.

For most of us, "cool" has a powerful appeal. There's much that's good which has become cool, and which is fantastic. But how much and to which particular cool we attach ourselves makes a big difference. Why do we like the particular cool? Is it because of how it makes us look, or because whatever it is, is something we truly like and see as good? What are our motivations when it comes to cool? A vital question. Cool for the wrong reasons is most decidedly not cool.

"The bullshit of 'too-cool-for school.' - Bullshit-manipulator-narcissists use rejection as a cudgel, whilst dangling the lure of approval and acceptance which won't ever be forthcoming, using these manipulations in their efforts to extort and bully."

Bullshitters have a confusing relationship with cool. Sometimes they're desperate for cool, other times they're the ones pushing cool. Either way, it's all bullshit. True cool cannot be manufactured, or staged, or used as a manipulation. No truly cool person would ever look down on others or exclude anyone maliciously.

Actually cool people care nothing for superiority and dominance, not to mention a complete unconcern with popularity and approval. Real cool people have independence-of-being. Bullshitters completely fail to understand what it means to be a real person, a person free from the opinions of others, a person with actual self-worth. They just can't comprehend a way-of-being which doesn't involve hierarchy and self-importance.

"The typical 'cool' is actually uncool, and real cool cares nothing about being cool."

Being "Helpful"

"Manipulation via 'helping' is well-disguised and not usually noticed."

The BMN likes to use the insidious tactic of pretending to be "helpful." They've come to understand the perception of "being helpful," is valuable. Beside the appearance of this, they have other motives. If one is the one providing the help, to the BMN this automatically means they're in a superior and dominant position. A position they will use to manipulate from, to obtain gains without scruple.

Their "being helpful" is just another way of being a bully. Under the guise of the appearance and image of helpfulness. Especially also because of their promotion as such. Many don't see the hidden agendas until too late. Sadly, they corrupt helpfulness and make many suspicious of help offered, with good reason. Discernment is needed concerning matters contaminated by the BMN. We can't assume most people are this way. BMNs are fortunately not the rule.

Good people are often led astray by their desire to be helpful. A tragedy. This happens when their motivations are focused on the helpful aspect of their actions and not the actions themselves. All too often it's appearing helpful, even for good people, that's the issue. Even worse, is when we help according to what *WE* believe and think is good and right, often completely ignoring what's appropriate for those we're trying to help. Helping alone isn't enough; it has to be *appropriate* helping, or we can make matters worse, not better.

"Are we a surface, a facade, or are we real? What are we? Our priorities define us."

Ch5 - Critical Obfuscation

"Like I said, we'll take your car.... mine's acting up. It's going to be a great trip! I thought we would split the cost. You owe me around $150 for the beers, snacks and chocolate I bought. Got a few stops we need to make as well. I'll tell you where to go when we get close. We'll share the driving after I have a nap. Let's go!"

Misdirection

"One of the chief tricks of bullshit-manipulator-narcissists is their ploy of misdirection, diverting attention away from the harmful bullshit, through use of tone, intimation, vibe, and other tactics."

Hiding what they're doing is of the utmost importance to the bullshitter. They *know* they're engaging in bullshit, sustained, extensive, and deliberate deception. Should this become clear, obvious, and refutable, and should what they say be proven to be false, their entire elaborate charade, their phoney edifice, will come tumbling down. A constant fear.

To guard against this calamity, they take great pains to *never* say anything definitive. Unless they absolutely have to. Their tactic to avoid being "called" on their nonsense is to always have it be unclear. They never say what they're trying to convey directly, clearly, or unambiguously; that's too risky.

They love using implication, innuendo, inference, intimation, suggestion, vibe, tone, and pushing a particular energy. These are all mechanisms which can't be easily pinned down, and thus they can't be held to them. Should matters not go as planned, they can quickly switch and pretend like nothing happened, or claim "it was all just a misunderstanding," and other such reversals of position. Their aim: to prevent being held responsible for anything they say or do.

Foisted Fog

"It is quite a feat uncovering a soul, and seeing what lies beneath the facade. Sometimes the facade is all there is."

Bullshitters *always* need to have an escape route, some way to be able to deny or excuse or explain, justify or otherwise reverse position. Thus obfuscation is a vital part of their strategy. Nothing is ever clear and upfront. Their enemy is focused consciousness and awareness.

If someone is alerted to what's happening, their game can't work. It relies on a subconscious inadvertent acceptance and going along with the subtle pressures and suggestions they constantly put out. They rely on their innuendos and implications simply being taken in by default and thereby acquiesced to and agreed to without the other even fully realising what's transpiring. Or if they do, it's just a vague feeling that's usually too troublesome to deal with consciously.

Obfuscation is their great ally, as it allows them the confusion and unclarity from which to protest or correct matters should their bullshit be called or exposed. They can then mount a defense from within their undefined communication. Since nothing was clear, it all boils down to interpretation and subjective perception. Or so they like to believe.

They love vagueness because they think no one could conclusively prove what they do. Of course, anyone who realises what they're about doesn't need to "prove" anything. If they're sensible they will just avoid future interactions. Ironically, the BMNs don't realise others obfuscate them when it comes to interacting.

Fake Friendships

"The bullshit-manipulators push self-promotion to gain justification-of-self, attention, and compliant followers, 'fans,' an 'audience,' groupies, sycophants, etc. They need a constant new supply of 'hosts' to prey off of. Bullshit-manipulator-narcissists are parasites!"

Obfuscation is used in many ways. Friendships are one such disguise. True and real friendships aren't possible for the BMN. For one, the lack of honesty and integrity precludes such an eventuality. Then there's the matter of equality, even a more-or-less equality. This too cannot be. The BMN always has to be top-dog. Besides, they don't actually want real friendships, since they want matters all in their favour. This is always their aim. They want followers, groupies, admirers, and those they can dominate. They obfuscate these agendas under the guise of "friendship."

They will make "friends" with the lost and lonely, with the desperate, and always with those whom they deem to be less than them. And try with all their being to suck up and cosy favour and somehow get "in" with those they see as superior or better than them. One but needs to watch Animal Planet to observe this mentality and psychology clearly on display in most animal species which aren't solitary. The BMN is mindful however to obfuscate their agendas, using friendship as a cover.

Who are our friends, and why? Asking and checking is valuable, often leading to change. Knowing our friends, knowing why we're friends with them, and why they with us, matters. Bringing light to our relationships makes all the difference. Unawareness when it comes to our friends and relationships is how we get into trouble.

Hidden Motives

"Bullshit-manipulators work the 'technicalities' and the grey areas promising one thing, yet having the agenda for something that's personal and entirely different. This is ethically fraudulent. The fraud of intent is the bullshit. They promote themselves, seldom the activity or surface objective."

Never will they show nor declare their real intentions and agendas. Always, the BMN has to obfuscate, as their real agendas aren't legit, not kosher, and aren't defensible. They know this. They know they're perpetually bullshitting. They know their lives are a lie, and to prevent being caught out in this perpetual fraud, they have to disguise everything.

It doesn't take much to see what they're up to. Once one is aware that people can pretend to do things for surface reasons, but have their personal agendas which are different, and in the case of the BMN, it's almost always about self-promotion, dominance, or money in some way, then we can fairly easily see through their charades.

A most powerful technique for use with anyone is to simply ask earnestly and sincerely: "What's the motive here?" If we ask this, and ask it with the intent to answer that question, we get incredible insight. Seeing and identifying motives, noticing and becoming more aware of the motives of another reveals them, clarifies them, and enables us to relate appropriately.

"There is BS for the sake of BS, for exaggeration and embellishment, essentially to enhance or glamorise some fact or truth. Then there is bullshit-manipulation, whose aim is to hide, obfuscate, and change the facts to achieve their narcissistic goals. These involve manipulations detrimental to those preyed upon, usually making them inadvertently complicit to the very real unethical selling out of their approval, energy, and agreement."

We have to be careful how we define, view, or understand bullshit, which exists in great variety, for many reasons. Typically, "taking liberties with the truth" isn't seen as a serious transgression, and it's this very perception that the BMN uses to obfuscate their nefarious doings. For they *are* nefarious. Much more than we would like to believe.

An indication of the bullshit-manipulator-narcissist's internal obfuscation is, despite their obsession with image and status, they don't mind being seen as a *bit* of a bullshitter. Or, as they sell it, somewhat of a showman, or a promoter, or as "colourful," etc., or even under the guise of "ambitious." Whatever label works that mollifies the harshness of bullshit and allows them some leeway and okay-ness when it comes to their liberties with accuracy. Not the truth, but strategic accuracy. If pressed, they will come up with justifications along the lines of, "Well, I like to keep it interesting" and "Why be boring? I just spice things up a bit," and such like. But of course these are all obfuscations.

"Bullshit obscured by more bullshit, a spiral vortex into ever more absurdity."

BMNs don't just distort a "bit" they do so grossly, engaging in radical inaccuracy and untruth. Because it's all perpetrated in the fog of obfuscation, it's difficult for anyone to hold them responsible. They love to think this is oh so clever. Using charm and friendly energy to "sell" their bullshit, making it hard for most people to see past this surface shell, since they push it strongly and make it pleasant on the surface, they thus gain acquiescence to their doings. This energy of friendliness and charm is one of their main obfuscating weapons.

Selling Untruth

"Bullshit is the selling of an unethical agenda, convincing others of a squirrelly idea, not necessarily facts, by co-opting agreements."

A persistent theme of bullshitters is the perpetual attempt at converting truth into untruth. They wish to transform the awful truths of their lives into what they believe will benefit them. They truly think their bullshit will bring them value. In small ways it does, temporarily. It never lasts, cannot last, so they continually need more and more, the deceit feeding on itself. No matter how hard they try, they can't transform those truths with wishful substitutions.

The other false idea they labour under is believing that if only they can get others to agree with their lies, this would make the falsehood "true," and thereby obfuscate the fact that it's deceit. They never seem to get that bullshit is lying, unethical, and uncool, and thus counterproductive.

Honesty is so imperatively critical. The more we observe its lack, the more we realise how vital self-honesty is to happiness and sensibility. We know this, but sometimes it seems we forget how imperative truthfulness with ourselves is. Powerful reminders of the consequences when we don't insist on self-integrity are useful to pull us back onto the path of realness.

Pushing Energy

"The wall-of-energy that bullshitters push is an obfuscating mechanism used to get away with bullshit, because we aren't looking at the overall pattern."

Obfuscation via the wall-of-energy is a powerful tool in the arsenal of the BMN. A tactic difficult to define or describe, but, once we're aware, it's easier to recognise. The BMN will, when engaging with someone, push a large energy out. It's a kind of pressure, not negative pressure, but pressure nonetheless. It can take the form of friendliness, or intensity, or urgency, focus of some kind, anything to keep the attention directed on whatever the BMN wants it. It's not so much about the specific target as it's about *NOT* wanting attention to shift in unwanted directions. Like their falsity, their lack of genuineness, their other agendas, and so on.

Once we shift out of these bubbles-of-obfuscation and zoom out our awareness and attention, we easily see what bullshitters are up to. That wall-of-energy prevents our immediate understanding. It's like bullshitters literally put a wall between them and who they're interacting with, preventing a full view of them. This energy is difficult to pinpoint exactly, but if you find yourself in an interaction and not able to think clearly, not able to catch a pause to consider what's going on, not able to do anything but follow along, then likely you're being pressed by a wall-of-energy.

The entire point of the wall-of-energy is to co-opt our

inadvertent agreement and prevent any objections that may arise. Likely most of us have experienced this pressure from an over-pushy "hard" sales person. The BMN uses this exact same tactic, except what they're "selling" is their bullshit. Usually self-promotion of some kind.

"The wall-of-energy bullshitters impose is something felt, but not readily identified, and often misconstrued. Clinging to overt apparent 'positive' impressions and notions is problematic and leads to inadvertent condoning of crappy attitudes."

Sadly, dealing with the wall-of-energy requires us to go *against* our natural instincts of goodness and giving the benefit of the doubt. This the BMN relies on, exploiting our automatic tendency to trust and be positive if the environment cues and prompts those reactions from us. Thus they "lead" us with this pressure into acquiescing with their agendas. If we in this way inadvertently react positively to them, by *implication* we're then positively disposed toward them and give and inadvertent stamp of approval.

We've been manipulated into this co-opting of our positivity, doing so mostly out of the pure habit of reaction, and our innate politeness and courtesy, not because we're truly looking at the total person and giving a considered opinion and perspective. The wall-of-energy is to remove our option of choice, to pressure us into inadvertent agreements and approvals.

"Pushed energy" comes not only from individuals, but from societal mechanisms also. From any form of authority or influence. So often we adopt these intents and energies without realising. Knowing this mechanism, seeing it's usage in personal interactions, helps us with recognising those more subtle influences which we otherwise might inadvertently adopt.

Using "Vibe"

"A purported intent is communicated via a supposedly benign energy that masks and hides a corrupt agenda."

Their chief trick is using mood, tone, vibe, etc. for purposes of colouring their intent. The BMN knows that most of us tend to just believe what is. Usually what's being presented isn't different to what the person actually intends. Most people are usually honest. The BMN exploits this goodness in us, using the impression generated by what they push out to obfuscate their true intentions, and the lies and falsity of what they're about.

Once we understand the importance and necessity of obfuscation, we easily see the true agendas, which always involves hiding the awful truth. The BMN also uses negativity to obfuscate. Everything for the BMN is about *relative* value. They care nothing for real actual value; all they care about is being *relatively* "better." Thus, being *less* negative gives them that satisfaction.

They possess deep-seated negativity within themselves. Their entire psychology stems from this inner negativity, not liking who and what they are. To obfuscate this unjustifiable ugliness, they will push others in ways that cause them to behave negatively, for the sole purpose of then pointing a finger and claiming a relative superiority, thereby obfuscating their persistent inner negativity.

"When bullshit meets its preposterous-self, its maker, it cannot handle the truth and reverts to even greater pretence to cover this dreaded eventuality, an illusion trying to connect to a reality based on mis-beliefs, which cannot exist. 'If you put a fancy hat on nothing, it's still nothing."

Paying attention to what the BMN is doing from the perspective of obfuscation is extremely handy, as it always begs the question, "What are you trying to hide, and why?" Simply asking that question is usually enough to clue us in to what's going on when it comes to the deceptions of the BMN.

Clarity and Unclarity

"Lack of clarity is a clear sign of potential bullshit."

Obfuscation happens during or after the bullshit is put out. The mindset of the bullshitter doesn't like clarity in general. They don't like to be pinned down. If matters are made clear, it leaves them no opportunity for bullshit and opportunistic improvisation. Thus, typically, if one is in an arrangement or agreement of some kind with a bullshitter, there will usually be a lack of specifics and precision. Knowing this, it behooves us to make sure we know what we're in for, and not just assume the usual normal standards of decency, fairness, and good behaviour.

For instance, going on a road trip with a bullshitter. The arrangement is to split costs, and matters are left there. Our assumptions are that activities will be engaged in jointly. If there are specific interests each wishes to pursue, the other will in turn get to do what they want. In other words, we expect balance if our interests and desire to do certain activities aren't always the same. We assume a fair give and take, like where we will eat together and so on. Alternating preference.

The bullshitter, and the BMN in particular, doesn't have this perspective. They want things all their own way, not caring about your interests nor desires in the least. With most people, stipulating such details pre-emptively isn't required. With bullshitters and BMNs, this is a sad necessity, especially if we don't have full control in the situation. Like, for instance, we use their car, or something of that nature. Of course, it's best not to place oneself in situations of interacting with these psychologies. If interaction is necessary, we not only have to be aware, but take pre-emptive measures. Clarity, focus, and precision are powerful tools for limiting bullshit, manipulation, and exploitation.

"Coercing and manipulating negative behaviour out of others doesn't justify, validate, nor substantiate the originating negativity. Merely a way to obfuscate the source of their negativity. Lack of clarity keeps options open for the bullshitter, allowing them to shift positions later. Taking any kind of stand goes against their grain, as it commits them, forcing them to be responsible for their actions."

Ch6 - BS Entanglement and Promise

Particular Pressures

"The bullshit-manipulator activates energy-entanglement by setting the tone with their energetic demeanour, and coming in with an agenda of pre-determining your options and positions for you. A subtle attempt at coercion and manipulation which is unethical!"

How does the BMN co-opt us into some sort of alignment with them? They create a mood, a pressure, and a strong energy, which then requires massive effort to counteract. Because all their interactions involve implication, innuendo, intimation, suggestion, and other subtle influencing techniques, along with the ever-present obfuscation, there's nothing definite and concrete that provides a focus, making it difficult to object. A fog of co-opted agreement is created, wherein objecting becomes problematic, as there isn't anything specific or defined to disagree with or resist. This difficulty is counted on by the BMN.

The manipulation and coercion is achieved by default, by implication, as in, "Well, you didn't object, so you must agree." This isn't necessarily said specifically, but again, it's the implications our lack of objection or disagreement creates. The BMN will actively behave, act, and speak as if we are, in fact, agreeing with them, without saying so directly, again, making opposition exceedingly problematic. Mostly this happens just beyond our conscious realisation, because it's so vague, nebulous, and disguised. Typically, we're left with a disquieting feeling of wrongness in some way, but not quite sure what.

Our politeness is at issue. We can't allow our goodness to be misused. Our remedy lies in: appropriate-intolerance. When do we redraw the lines of the unacceptable? The time is now. When we become aware those lines have drastically shifted without our agreement, without us noticing, we have to act.

Condoning Complicity

"Bullshit-manipulators DO something to the unsuspecting, which is the conspiracy-of-complicity. They knowingly conscript condoning of their crappiness."

That fog of implication is used to conscript our inadvertent agreement, making us unwitting accomplices to their bullshit. The BMN is always pushing an untruth, attempting to sell a lie, the lie of what they are. This deception is typically accompanied by promise. Sometimes those promises are overtly stated, but mostly implied and suggested only. They use this subverted agreement to cultivate their false persona, using our co-opted acquiescence to influence others and create the impression they desire. In this way they leverage our honesty and goodness, especially in situations where a third party knows us, and now it appears we approve of the BMN. They take this as an endorsement of sorts, even though it all happens without the application of any conscious attention.

We have to be aware and vigilant of these subtle entanglements with the bullshit. We often end up seemingly supporting what we do not. Once entangled in this way, the only way out is to specifically deny or counteract the BMN by deliberately saying something negative about them. This is difficult, because of the obfuscations, vagueness and general fuzziness of the bullshit, pinning down exactly what they do is difficult. Once we're aware, it makes it difficult for the BMN to implement this nonsense in the first place.

"The entanglement bullshitters foist is a subtle interpersonal dynamic which they exploit. A parasitic entanglement born out of inadvertent complicity."

We can't allow ourselves to be a party to the bullshit-manipulator-narcissist's bullshit and lies. We can't be co-opted to be complicit in this forgery of self. We can't allow ourselves to, by implication, condone this way-of-being, to validate their thoroughly unscrupulous and unethical persona.

A big deal, because all the public BMNs we see so often in politics or other influential positions, started off in somebody's day-to-day world where they weren't thwarted, stopped, objected to, and otherwise not enabled through awareness and understanding. We all wish to change the world, and we can. It starts with each of us doing our small part. Refusing to enable bullshit is one such powerful way of changing the world, one bullshitter at a time. Otherwise we're complicit, by allowing our entanglement with this pervasive problem.

"The Truth does not require your participation in order to exist. Bullshit does." - Terence McKenna

Assumed Ownership

"For some mindsets, they take ownership not just of things, but people. Even when discarded, they still assume 'territorial rights' over these people and their long past relationships. How preposterous!"

Relationships with a BMN are especially problematic, and if we're unfortunate enough to fall into one, getting out is troublesome. That massive entanglement they continually foster makes un-entangling difficult. The BMN sees a partner in a relationship as "theirs," as a possession, as something they control, whether this is the actuality or not. It's how it is internally for the BMN, which makes being in a relationship with them completely untenable.

Likewise, BMNs like to take ownership of anything they can, as a way of asserting control and power and to "prove" their status and wonderfulness. Especially popular is anything they can use to show off with and enhance their image and status, whether they have claim to it or not

The only remedy, once we become aware we're involved with a BMN, is to end all interaction. Everything. No more contact. For even after the relationship is ended, the BMN will still try to assert some form of control or possession. It's difficult to imagine the preposterousness of this if not personally experienced, but amazingly it's so. If we just could've seen it coming.

"One seeks to take power, the other gives it away. The

lesson for both is the same. It's for each to stand in their own power... Take control of your own being, live in your own inner power, and the need to control or be controlled will leave you."

Deep profound words going beyond the scope of this book, but worthy to be mindful of. If we don't wise up, we're part of the problem. We can't claim ignorance as an excuse forever. Through this book, we'll have the power to recognise, and thus understand, helping us to avoid bullshitters and BMNs. Or, when we do have to interact, we'll be aware, our awareness alone a powerful limiting effect on their bullshit.

Ch7 - Comparison and Hierarchy

Better Than

"The bubble of the relativity-mindset believes it can make an actual negative situation appear positive by comparison."

What's comparison and hierarchy about? The comparative-mindset and the superiority paradigm. Everything in the bullshit psychology is shaped by those two concepts. How they compare relatively is of supreme importance to the bullshitter, especially so for the BMN. They have no concern with acquiring absolute value. It matters only where they are in the hierarchy. "Better than" and relative status is important, not, being good for its own sake. The value of goodness lies only in expediency.

This obsession with relative value is what leads them to

the manipulations, put-downs, and pull-downs. They like to think they're the "best," but they know on an objective basis this is absurd, so they settle for being the local "best," which usually means that they find somebody to dominate in some way. It's so utterly pathetic, but it's a reality. Their lives are made miserable by this constant comparing, by their preoccupation with hierarchy. They can't just enjoy themselves being themselves.

These self-evaluations are always relative to others, never absolute to their own standards and goals. Relative objectives and values are problematic; the bullshitter can only ever be as good as who they compare themselves to. When the self is fake, what gets compared? It's why independence-of-being is so critical, otherwise one ends up a slave of comparison.

"Decency isn't necessarily innate, as a consequence some end up enjoying being negative, a result of the necessity for gross ego to make the constant effort of maintaining the delusion of superiority. It's easier to pull down others than it is to raise the self."

Dominance

The short-cut mentality is a large part of this mindset. They want to be "better" and superior. It's a huge deal to them. Being so in any real sense takes energy and effort, an effort they're reluctant and unwilling to make, as they don't believe they can actually succeed, so they have to find alternative means to satisfy this ego-craving. The easiest is simply to pull others down below them. Or, as with chickens, to "peck on their heads." With human interactions, this "pecking" is a variety of negative acts.

"Controlling a situation doesn't require dominating anyone and overstepping the boundaries of respect and

humanity. All that's necessary is being in charge of oneself. Trying to bully or manipulate others is merely a substitute for lack of personal solidity. Dominance and control aren't necessarily the same, with neither being integral to real leadership."

Bullshitters are far from feeling in command of themselves. How can they be if their self is a lie? That falseness corrupts everything they do, and sadly they believe the solution lies in dominating, or being "higher" or "better" than others. The idea of simply being happy and content within themselves is utterly foreign to them. Unfortunately.

"The top-dog, bottom-dog mindset is an assessment evaluation of relative positioning, perceived status, and image, in an attempt to establish superiority and hierarchy."

Primitive Psychology

Bullshitters, and especially BMNs, suffer from a primitive mindset and logic. If we look at the animal kingdom, we see the same behaviours of dominance and bullying, and valuation placed on physical prowess and appearance. The logic of value in the primitive animal perspective is all superficial. Deeper values, like honesty, sensibility, integrity, strategy, and thinking aren't valued. Dominance is purely based on either being bigger or more aggressive. When those aren't options, the bullshitter relies on "looking the part," pretending to "have the goods."

The basic attributes which result in dominance within the primitive-animal logic have generally been substituted by humans. Yes, there are still instances where physical bullying takes place, and many are valued for their looks alone, but in general these have been replaced by actual relevant capabilities. Some have realised the actual skills and abilities aren't needed. Others just have to *believe* those abilities and skills exist.

Thus, we get to bullshit. It's an attempt at dominance, being in control, having value, being a "leader," and otherwise securing some benefit for themselves by pretending to have what others seek. If we look closely, bullshitters always sell an image, a generalised idea they can deliver on their promises. Never selling specifics as to how exactly. They just create the impression they can, usually based on selling confidence in some way. Why a con is called a con. It's all based on pushing confidence.

Bullshitters sell the confidence of having value, of being the dominant one. When in positions of dominance, besides the ego pay-offs, they know pushing their bullshit is easier, as they can shut down questioning. They know many are happy to follow without thinking. They exploit this laziness and lack of personal responsibility. Hierarchy and dominance thus have additional value besides ego-boosting. When bullshitters do find themselves in positions of authority, their main commandment is always "Thou shalt not question!"

"The comparative-mindset and lack of self-honesty limits truly relating."

How can a bullshit being relate? How can a false, fake, imaginary, and thus unreal personality and character relate? It can't. It's like having a relationship with someone in a movie. Not possible. Since the desire for hierarchy is so central to bullshitters as it facilitates their bullshit and fakeness, and because part of the self-bullshit is that it's only *relative* superiority which is needed, these mindsets are always comparing.

They constantly compare to everything, to see where they are. If they're substantially "lower" in their estimation, they will do everything they can to suck up, gain favour, impress and otherwise try to attach themselves in a way they believe will bring them advantage. Or failing that, they will try to pull down those above them. When higher, they will seek to dominate and entrench this relative superiority. They're fundamentally insecure, because how can one be secure when everything about the self is false and fake?

This constant comparing makes relationships impossible. If they compare, and the other is seen to be "better" than them, they feel like crap relatively. It's absurdly foolish. Instead of enjoying the value of the other, they turn it into feeling bad by comparison.

This results in them needing to pull the other down to gain relative superiority. If they succeed, they lose any perception of value in the other, typically turning negative toward them as they then see the other as worthless. The comparative-mindset, when combined with the belief in the importance of hierarchy, ends in a complete lose-lose, no-possibility-of-win situation. A foolishness beyond compare.

Sociology of Pecking

"Pecking-order hierarchy has no ethics."

We might ask why bullshitters don't strive to self-improve? In pecking order logic, position in the hierarchy is established by whose head one can peck on. Purely an activity of putting down others. There's no place for goodness or actual improvement which doesn't serve dominance. The entire psychology of pecking is geared to seeing who can be pecked, how one puts them down, keeps them down.

Pecking is exclusively a relative and comparing mindset. In chicken-land, independent individuality isn't a possibility. It's either peck or be pecked upon. Enjoyment of the self, as an activity unrelated to hierarchy is unknown. An impossible concept when everything is only about hierarchy and pecking.

"A chicken-mindset in a human is an unspeakable tragedy."

Conventionality

When we look at the hierarchical and comparative-mindset we also see how utterly dependent they are on convention. They're slaves to "should." So terrified are they of the perceived negative consequences of disapproval, so completely do they buy into the idea personal value can *ONLY* be found through superiority and dominance, that they believe the "system" they're in is the only option. This translates into these mindsets being extremely conventional. They seek to maintain and cling to the status quo because it's familiar.

They know how to deal with hierarchy, they know pecking, they know dominance, they know superiority, they know bullshit. Anything they don't know, is threatening. The unknown is where they have no competence, no skill, no ability, and thus no power. Already they're substantially insecure in the known, the unknown is exponentially worse.

One can't possibly dominate and be "higher" in areas where one doesn't know. This is why change, innovation, learning and growth, thinking, science, anything which threatens the stability of the status quo and established convention, is feared and disliked intensely, and energetically resisted.

With the entire being of the bullshitter founded on a hollow lie, any potential disruption or exposure of that lie is a huge threat. Anything new is such a threat, since unknown, it's not within the sphere of control. This doesn't mean bullshitters can't embrace the new. They can, and do, but only if they believe it gives them an "edge." Only if they believe it gives them some sort of superiority. So focused are they on all the complexity needed to maintain their bullshit and their false lives and personas, they have little time, energy, or ability to learn and grow. Any adoptions of the new are typically superficial only, as is everything in their lives.

"The life of a fool is a foolish business indeed."

Being aware of and understanding the comparison-mindset and hierarchy are essential for understanding bullshit. If we look around ourselves, at our own lives and interactions, we often see these mechanisms in play, to various degrees. How much we subscribe to them defines us and reveals us. What's really of value? Being better or being good? A question we need to ask, need to understand, need to hold in awareness, as the difference is profound.

Ch8 - Distorted Beliefs and Delusions

"He's applying for the 'King of the Jungle' position. Says he has ruled the last 3 jungles he has lived in, commands respect, gets the job done and is ruthless when needed. I kinda like him!"

Distorted Self-Belief

"To have someone on the world stage in our face like this is truly a blessing in disguise... how awesome to see this in action, as the mirror of it does seem to be having good side consequences in terms of awakening to BS."

The bullshitter in question, so prominent on TV and social media, is indeed a gift of awareness. An exemplification of that myth of personal belief: *"All you need is to believe in yourself."* No! It's movie bullshit. Clearly, one needs much more. This myth is a particularly devastating one, enabling all sorts of gross incompetence and inappropriateness, and especially, promoting severe overestimation of self, to dangerous levels. I don't care how much you may believe you can do brain surgery, you won't be testing your theory on me! It's absurd of course, in any field other than, it seems, in politics.

"All you need is to believe in yourself."

The problem here is that "all." That misleading "all you need…" A recurring theme of many movies and a huge measure of their popularity. Also, a source of fodder for much bullshit via distortion. These movies take the common man and show how he, too, could be a hero, enabling the bullshitter's myth that no talent, no skills, no abilities etc. can be morphed into huge success simply by virtue of the magic of self-belief.

But, of course, even in the movies, and Stallone's movies come to mind here, the characters *do* acquire skills, and *do* make huge efforts. This is conveniently not focused on too much by the lazy and incompetent, and by bullshitters who are so adamantly desirous of a shortcut to the greatness they believe is their due. The "simply believe in yourself" theme is another short-cut mis-belief contorted by bullshit.

Tricks

"Short-cuts? Short-cuts based on nothing, are nothing but short-cuts to nowhere."

One such Stallone movie which features the self-belief myth is Over The Top. It's not necessary to be familiar with the movie, it's simply a convenient mechanism to illustrate many of the concepts in this book. The movie itself doesn't push the bullshit; it's a distortion of elements in the movie. These corruptions are highly significant when it comes to the distorted beliefs of bullshitters. Just to be clear, belief in oneself is a highly important component when it comes to pretty much anything, but it's *a* component, not the *only* component.

There's more which fuels the BS mythology in the movie. It revolves around one of these BS myths, the myth of the "trick" or the "secret move." The hero is a truck-driving arm-wrestler who has real skill and ability. Early in the movie already he's seen working out, putting effort into furthering his ability. He constantly works out, even while driving. He also has a "trick." Two of them really. Not the biggest fellow by far, but he has two potent win-against-all-odds "tricks." First, the magical hat:

Lincoln Hawk: *"What I do is I just try to take my hat and I turn it around, and it's like a switch that goes on. And when the switch goes on, I feel like another person, I feel, I don't know, I feel like a... like a truck. Like a machine."*

The aim here isn't to disparage psychological self-leverage, which has enormous value. Point is, *in itself,* this trick is obviously not enough. It's a *motivational* technique to maximise the practised and developed skills and abilities. The bullshitter sees only the trick. To them it represents a means of short-cutting directly to "win." This notion has inordinate appeal. They believe their bullshit is such a "trick," which enables them to transform into a different person. In a sense it does, but it's a fake person, one unable to do much of anything, because, well, they're not real.

The other "trick" our arm-wrestling hero has is a special "move" of repositioning his hand during the crucial stage of an arm-wrestling match, whereby his hand goes "over the top" of his opponent's. Again, like magic, he becomes invincible. This hand move literally represents a special leverage over another, resulting in a "win." Forgotten is the very real inordinate and enormous effort our hero is making. The massive stress and strain, coupled with intense focus, immersion, concentration, persistence, and determination fall by the wayside. The "move" is all that's remembered. Bullshitters love these "moves," especially "moves" which give them leverage over others. They're constantly on the lookout for anything which represents a magic get-something-for-nothing ability.

There's an irony to the movie being called "Over the Top," as this is precisely the definition of bullshitters, but this movie is by no means responsible for the bullshit mindset. These myths, and similar, are common, not only in Hollywood, but in popular culture throughout the ages. It's convenient to see them all so neatly packaged into one movie.

Anti-Smarts

"An acute awareness of our own nincompoopery is a critical ingredient for self-development."

The movie is full of myths. Like the intellectual myth and the dislike of intellectualism conveyed via the obnoxious, but intelligent, military school cadet son, who spouts and repeats some nonsense about "social scale" and "mental age." Of course, the movie's hero, the dad, a truck driver of "perhaps a mental age of eleven," is irritated by this, and being the cool Stallone, disproves these ideas just by being him, and the hero of the movie. "You don't read much do you?" the son further indicts the father.

The implication, via the hero, heavily implied, is one doesn't need "smarts" to be successful. Even though the hero is certainly no eleven-year-old mentally. He takes great pride in his son's intelligence. The anti-smarts myth and beliefs are confusing and full of contradictions. Typical of many bullshitter myths.

Bullshitters especially like anti-intellectual myths. Or the myth that "smarts" don't matter. They're too lazy to make any effort to acquire any real abilities and competence and want to cheat their way to everything, so these myths are convenient to them. Especially since they know how far behind they really are. All as a result of the continual bullshit pretending and refusing to actually learn anything. The result of their bullshit is **anti-smart** indeed. Their own.

Myths of Convenience

"Credo of the narcissist: 'If I want it, it's right.'"

Conflict between myths is common with bullshitters. Like being anti-intellectual, anti-smarts, but also making every effort they can to appear smart or intelligent. They will take pride in their own cleverness whenever they can, and of anyone with whom they're associated, all the while disparaging any kind of intelligence which doesn't reflect well on them.

The myths most suitable in a situation are adopted then dropped as needed, instantly substituted with another convenient myth. Even if it contradicts. Truth and consistency matter not. The bullshit distortion and utilisation of popular conceptions to suit the needs of the moment is a go-to mechanism of the bullshitter. If it serves their purpose, the purpose of short-cutting, that's all they care about.

Over The Top is a decent enough movie, despite its failings, like massive errors of logic, common also to the bullshitter. The movie is a fantastic metaphor to represent bullshit and the bullshitter. They, too, ignore inconvenient truths. For the climax of the movie, the hero enters the world arm-wrestling championship, a *double elimination* tournament. We're reminded of this repeatedly. All to set up the hero's first loss and providing the opportunity for the son to **feed back** the father's earlier pep-talk about believing in oneself.

The hero then goes on, in the climax, to defeat the *undefeated* five-year champion, Bull Hurley, and crowned the "winner." The fact of our hero needing to defeat the undefeated champion *twice* is conveniently overlooked. Utter bullshit. It's symptomatic of bullshit and bullshitters. They just as easily overlook inconvenient or unpleasant facts. Their personal mythology of deception is much the same as the Hollywood myth falseness. It's all about how the movie sells, not how realistic nor sensible it is. It's all about the "optics," all about how it "looks."

The flaw for the bullshitter is in movies, often or mostly, we overlook these flaws. Movies are escapist entertainment. We willingly allow the nonsense, knowing it's bullshit. What the bullshitter doesn't realise, or doesn't want to acknowledge, is the myth of pretend, Hollywood style, doesn't apply or work in real life, with real people. This doesn't deter them from trying to make the myth of bullshit a reality.

Validations

"Achieving a bullshit goal cannot result in satisfaction."

The movie has more myths, such as, subtly, the hero isn't above bending morality nor ethics slightly when needed, like when he hustles another arm-wrestler into a bet. Mixed messages. The hero needs to be "relatable." That great crime Hollywood perpetrates where they legitimise and condone otherwise objectionable behaviour. These validations of behaviours which aren't exactly bad, but aren't exactly good either, is Hollywood's bullshit. The bullshitter seizes upon these validations to legitimise their own transgressions, which are much more egregious.

What sticks in the mind of the general movie-goer about the movie is the repeated focus on the core "gimmicks." Those two "tricks" which enable the key component of success against all odds. For the bullshitter this is a powerful validation of their mindset. Their "trick," their gimmick, is bullshit. For the bullshitter, these tricks, and cheating, are one and the same. They conveniently overlook the effort part. Belief in self is there to enable the self to learn, not to replace learning. A distinction the bullshitter makes every effort to ignore.

"If I have the belief that I can do it, I shall surely acquire the capacity to do it even if I may not have it at the beginning." - Mahatma Gandhi

Looking Good

Impulsive, reckless, and emotionally fuelled behaviour to "prove" how caring and what an actually good guy the hero is, is a common part of such movies. In this case the hero drives his truck through the gate, over the fountain, and into the mansion where his son is. To retrieve him, guaranteeing losing him through legitimately being arrested. More bullshit. But it makes the hero "look good." A "radical" move, which looks "cool." Another flawed myth.

The bullshit is in real life, the hero suffers real detrimental consequences, often for a lifetime. Bullshitters seize on these behaviours, but they adapt them to make a show only, making gestures which seem like they really care, but don't. Bullshitters are intimately connected to such movie and popular beliefs. They see how it works to make the hero "look good." The Hollywood myth is all about enhancing how the hero appears. This is all the bullshitter cares about. They thoroughly buy into this mindset and belief, focusing in on only this aspect, translating it into their obsession: self-promotion.

"It's not how they look or what they say; it's what they do. Promises mean nothing until delivered."

Stupid-Winning

Another overlooked aspect of movie logic the bullshitter distorts to support their bullshit is heroes of this type do stupid things in these movies, but somehow the movie makes it all good. Despite the foolishness of the hero, he comes out on top. The bullshitter clings to this myth with all their worth, because they've given up on real personal-development and learning long ago, and are thus severely limited.

Bill had taken his bullsh!t to new levels over the last 12 months basing every decision and every action on the main character '*Ace McStrong*' from the movie '*King of the Boardroom*'.

Bill's world fell apart with the surprise release of '*King of the Boardroom 2 - The complete ruin and disgrace of Ace McStrong*'. Through his tears, he pondered which fake character he could be next!

They hold tight to this myth, the myth they can triumph despite their lack of ability. Sadly, their belief in the myth of bullshit only serves to entrench what they run away from. Despite their ignorance and incompetence, but with every act of bullshit which hides and disguises these uncomfortable facts, bullshitters further distance themselves from real learning and growth.

Bob "Bull" Hurley: "*I drive truck, break arms, and arm wrestle. It's what I love to do, it's what I do best. Being number one is everything. There's no second place. Second sucks.*"

This myth, that "winning is everything," is a particularly destructive belief. In the movie, Bull Hurley is also the bully, the somewhat bad guy nemesis, the guy who "does whatever it takes" to win. A mindset and belief particularly suited to the bullshitter. Ethics and scruples are inconveniences not suited to the "winner." Aggression, nastiness, meanness, all are inadvertently legitimised by this myth, particularly with impressive bad guy "winners" such as Bull Hurley.

"The inordinate belief that 'winning is everything' causes a distorting immersion of perspective."

The bullshitter's beliefs of dominance and superiority are particularly served by such characters and movie myths. Myths the bullshitter lives by. They're careful to hide these negative appearing practises. A core component of their bullshit is to always be the "nice guy" hero. They love having all these underhanded "tricks" at their disposal, and like being the bully. They will use negativity whenever they can "get away" with it, as negativity and bullying are an easy shortcut to dominance. The bullshitter, particularly, will much rather be, to them, the "real" winner, the Bull Hurley, the natural bully, rather than the once-in-a-lifetime freak winner like the "good guy" hero of the movie Over The Top.

"The indoctrination that winning is the only option leads to much self-bullshit, all to substantiate and justify lack of integrity."

Of course the hero's win is over the top, the bullshitter is acutely aware of bullshit, and the hero's win is highly unlikely in most real-world scenarios. Thus they aspire to be the more realistic "winner:" the bully!

The movie so aptly represents the actuality of the bullshitter, as they, too, are over the top in real life, constantly crossing boundaries of decency and ethics. All the while appearing nice and "looking good." But, on closer examination, aren't good at all.

"The belief that 'winning is the be-all-and-end-all' is what corrupts ethics, character, and integrity, because it justifies, at-all-costs. The 'win-at-all-costs' mindset is a huge contributing factor to bullshit, particularly self-bullshit. Winning has come to represent justification."

Psychology

"Know others, to know thyself."

When it comes to knowing the psychology of others, we can know what's going on inside, through various means, which of course don't include being inside another's head. We can gather much from observing behaviour, from inference, extrapolation, implication, and such tools. Yes, one might argue, but how can you ever know for certain you're correct? One cannot with absolute certainty, and this applies to everything, but...

When we can *predict* with a high degree of accuracy the behaviour of others, we can have a measure of confidence in our psychological assessments. Our aim when it comes to bullshit is to be able to know bullshit well enough to be able to predict bullshitters, allowing us to be ahead of their games.

Also, an acute self-understanding in this is an invaluable tool. We can use ourselves and our thorough understanding of our own psychology to gain insight into others. Especially if we've pursued a psychology of mindset experimentation and remember the many and varied paths we followed, particularly those we were temporarily immersed in, those dead-ends of being, and what all we did when so consumed. Understanding our own bullshit, however small, helps us understand gross bullshit.

"Wanting to 'transcend others' is an ambition that's oxymoronic! You don't transcend others; you transcend yourself! Relative improvement doesn't necessarily mean actual improvement!"

In all of psychology there's a kind of logic at play, one determined by the immersive context, the logic which applies only inside the limited bubble-of-awareness. Once this is understood, figuring out the psychologies of others is really not that difficult, including that of the bullshitter.

Combine all of this with a thorough understanding of cause and effect, especially as it applies to motivation, goals, intent, beliefs, especially beliefs, then it becomes a relatively straightforward business to know another's psychology. It seems tricky, but not really. Naturally, all assumptions are, and stay, assumptions until verified through observable behaviour.

Knowing Others

"Insisting on an untruth just doesn't work. It short circuits."

It's difficult to comprehend or even imagine what's going on in a field where we're not expert. When it comes to psychology, this is particularly problematic, as most of us regard ourselves expert to some degree when it comes to "knowing people." Typically a false belief. One though, which isn't well received at all if actually shown and demonstrated to be untrue. It leads to large measures of resentment and retaliatory criticism, and unfortunately for many, "feeling stupid" by comparison.

The loss of the feeling of competence when it comes to human understanding is one not easily accepted. We mention this because it's a particular problem in these matters. Like spotting liars, we all like to believe we can do so easily, but many tests and studies have shown the actual fallacy of this belief. Here, awareness of the underlying mechanisms of bullshit comes in handy. Making the effort to truly understand all that's involved is well worth the time and energy.

"Somehow, for whatever reason, when it comes to new relationships, three months seems to be the magic time limit for maintaining pretence."

We need to be humble in the assessment of our ability to assess others. Not making snap judgements nor going exclusively by our gut and first impressions. These are often completely wrong, especially when it comes to bullshitters. They've mastered the art of making good initial impressions. We especially have to know and understand once we form a definite opinion about another, we tend to stick with that opinion. Usually long past the point where it's obviously no longer true.

If we can develop the habit of withholding forming an opinion of others, we will protect ourselves from falling into this psychological trap. We can prevent all the problems of becoming entangled with bullshitters in the first place by reserving our involvements with people in general until we know more. When we do become involved, to do so strategically, gradually, giving relationships time to grow and build, allowing plenty time to pay attention and observe. Our good opinions of others is a precious resource, not to be squandered willy-nilly simply as a reflex so we can be seen as "nice" people. Being sensible and good is much more important than appearing to be a nice person.

"Arrogance is a quicksand of the soul! A dead-end of being!"

Setting aside our own nonsense is of particular importance when it comes to understanding bullshit and the bullshitter. Particularly when it involves a major determining aspect of their psychology: the delusion they constantly manufacture to keep their silliness going.

Delusion is tricky to understand from the outside. The delusion of the bullshitter is a constant disguise of the truth, an inner state maintained via immersion into their various convenient self-supporting myths and mis-beliefs. They use distortion of popular and even sensible beliefs to maintain this deliberate illusion. Problem is, psychological perversions of this nature rely on a limiting of awareness to exist. It's this aspect of self-deception which is hard to observe and makes understanding delusion somewhat difficult.

"The ego-maniac is obsessed with their unrealistic unsupported fantasy of superiority, resulting in a gross distortion of perception, creating the delusion necessary for reconciling this contradiction."

We observe a bullshitter, and they have intelligence, they have the *ability* to understand and behave normally. They're clearly not asylum material, making it difficult to believe they will act and behave in ways which severely limit them. Yet this is exactly what they do. Their bullshit does precisely this, limiting truth to only what's convenient. Likewise limiting awareness to what's convenient. They go even further, distorting awareness and truth to what's desirable. This insistence on their particular and chosen version of reality is the delusion they live in.

"To truly understand madness, we have to be crazy ourselves."

Understanding the delusion of the bullshitter is greatly helped by understanding how desperately they *want* their bullshit to be true. It absolutely *has* to be true for them, they've dug themselves in too deep to turn back, to let go of the lies. It would mean they effectively have to start their lives over, becoming children again, so much have they skipped and neglected. Starting over, in the mind of the bullshitter, would be starting at the bottom, a horror of an impossibility. This disaster, to them, they will under no circumstances allow. Their delusion has to be maintained at all costs.

When we look closely and truly come to understand the bullshitter, the answer is yes to the question, are they crazy? They are, it's a functional madness, well hidden. Their inner world of delusional necessity is a different reality from the bullshit persona they project to the world. This enormous difference is one of the largest obstacles to understanding the bullshitter. It's hard to believe such a vast difference of being can co-exist in one person. We cannot allow ourselves to be fooled by our primary senses, by what *appears* to be repetitively normal and benign. This is the illusion which, if believed, makes *us* a bit delusional in turn.

"Often times we just don't want to know."

Over-Estimation

"Bullshit-manipulators grossly over-estimate themselves, pushing unjustified confidence, even considering themselves suitable for a job or project they're wholly unsuited to, all because of their delusional desires. To sycophants who contribute to the delusion, the bullshit might sound good, but the price paid is steep indeed. Bullshit-manipulators already have a vocation: self-promotion, making them ineffectual for anything else."

Despite repeated indications to the contrary, or perhaps because of their perceived negative inner-reality, the bullshitter clings to the belief and idea they can do, or are capable of doing, anything. This isn't a self-belief rooted in their ability to learn. Unfortunately not. This fantasy develops from the mis-beliefs fostered by their overblown egos. When an opportunity presents, they will promote themselves, not as potentially being able to do something they know absolutely nothing about, but as someone who *already* knows more than enough. An incredible consequence of their mis-beliefs combined with their arrogance and delusion. Their confidence lies not in their ability to learn or adapt, but in their ability to bullshit their way through whatever may come.

Needless to say, they don't last long, usually. Their utter inability to meet their promises ends up as nothing in the long run. Learning and adapting with a view to avoid the mistake of over-selling themselves and over-promising doesn't seem to be an option. This behaviour isn't rooted in strategic sober thinking. Their immersion into their self-created delusion causes them to simply *react* whenever an opportunity arises. There's a part which grabs at the offer for its benefits and rewards, mostly that immediate thoughtless reaction is simply a desperate grab for attention and approval.

When they respond to an offer or opening, by implication they're stating they're the *kind* of person who can do what's required. To the unsupported ego of the bullshitter, even claiming, by implication, relatively simple skills is a big deal. They get instant "status" as someone who can do. In this, their perceptions are those of the inner child they still are, having skipped learning because of constantly replacing growth with bullshit. Grabbing childishly at any potential position or task gives them the immediate "shine" from the implied, "I can do this."

When children behave this way, we smile, and usually it costs us nothing but a supporting attitude as they learn. But in otherwise supposedly mature adults who also know they're bullshitting, this is a costly deception. If the bullshitters were to not actually go through with their silliness, that would still be somewhat okay, if perhaps tiresome. They have no scruples whatsoever in positioning themselves where they have absolutely no business being, and they often cause much harm and ill-consequence with their bullshit and incompetence.

"The insistence on gross arrogance looking to manufactured rightness and not actual rightness is rooted in denigration. 'Imitation and pretence' is just another dupe! And self-dupe. The illusion and delusion is covert and overt."

Using their arrogance as a kind of weapon is of great use to a bullshitter. Manipulation is so much easier when accompanied by the pressure of an unassailable confidence. But confidence without any backing, is simply arrogance. We see arrogance, the bullshitter sees confidence. So great can be their mis-beliefs in themselves, in how they "should" be in positions they have absolutely no place being, they exude a hard to assail air of belonging. Often they can convince others who pay attention only to attitude and primitive posturing they not only belong where they aren't in the least qualified to be, but are actually doing a good job when they aren't. The infecting power of bullshit on those who swallow is mighty.

Accomplices

"Getting others to join flawed attitudes and behaviour in an attempt to 'prove' 'rightness' is a function of lack of integrity."

Bullshit-manipulator-narcissists sometimes hone their manipulation skills to the extent they can trap others into being their bullshit accomplices. First they will manipulate their way into a situation which involves others. Then they will promote and promise, to everyone at large, what benefits those in it with them. Once those benefits of perception are realised by their unwitting accomplices, as the false promises are believed by the public or customers, their 'fish' are hooked. They've created an illusion to the greater community or public. An illusion which forces their inadvertent allies, who were manipulated into being followers, via the bullshit promises and assertions made on their behalf, into supporting the bullshitter.

This bullshit naturally seldom comes close to happening as promised, and now these followers and perhaps reluctant supporters are forced into the shared delusion. They have to join. If they don't, they risk bursting the bubble. The consequence of which is to expose them as being the dupes they are for having gulped at the bullshit, never mind feasting greedily. Looking like the right idiots they were is a thoroughly unacceptable option. The BMN has an especially easy time manipulating other bullshitters with large egos.

"Emotional pressure and bullying to get people to like, approve, accept, think, and treat one as special or important is a short-sighted self-defeating shortcut."

Inside the delusion, manipulating the perceptions of others is a necessity, all to prevent that always threatening implosion. No matter how hard they try, bullshit always comes back to bite the bullshitter, the longer they get away with their crap, the more severe and devastating that bite. They also know this. When they see that impending collapse approaching, they will become ever more dangerous.

Old African hunter's wisdom has the *wounded* buffalo as the most dangerous animal in Africa. When wounded, the buffalo will turn not only mean, but aggressively vindictive and persistent in its efforts to cause harm to its attackers. Bullshitters, and particularly the bullshit-manipulator-narcissist, become especially dangerous when desperate.

As their falseness and lies become ever more obvious, their bullshit escalates to ever-increasing ridiculousness. Since further bullshit is their only option, they will keep doubling-down, going to extreme lengths to self-preserve. They will burn down the entire world to deny their attackers any survival.

They care not for anything but the preservation of their delusion, even if it means destroying what's also valuable to them. A collapsing vanity-self, which knows its doom is near, rampages with abandon, intent only on causing harm and pain. Beware indeed that most dangerous of creatures, the mortally wounded ego.

"Self-bullshit and bullshitting others has bullshitters think they can change the truth. They want so desperately to believe they can transform untruth into truth."

Based on What?

"Fickle-shits think and pretend their fickleness isn't perceived by others just because it's not commented on."

When attempting to extricate themselves from the consequences of their actions, bullshitters will intensely "push" their bullshit. Becoming intent on convincing others their lies are true. They won't present their false reality, or "narrative," as speculation, as a maybe or a what-if, no, they will boldly state their bullshit as fact. Usually invoking some nebulous assumed proof like "studies have shown," or substituting some other vague authority. All we have to do to spot this bullshit is ask ourselves whose word we're being asked to believe, and based on what exactly. With bullshit, we usually don't have to look too deep, to spot the hollowness.

Another tactic they use to push their bullshit is repetition. Over and over they will push their "story," believing, and desperately hoping, this repetition will eventually make their bullshit true. When they repeat, especially repeat with emphasis and insistence, we get a clue into what they fear, what they're frantic to conceal. Once we come to know bullshit, bullshitters are absurdly transparent. We just have to cross that hurdle of believing someone so absurd and obvious can actually exist, let alone actually behave with such preposterousness so repeatedly. The question is, how repeatedly are we going to refuse to believe, refuse to acknowledge, refuse to understand?

"Some are so insistent on their indulgence - at all costs, resulting in self-deception, deception, delusion."

We become complicit in maintaining the delusion the bullshitter makes so much effort to push when we simply accept their "assertions of fact" as actual fact. How does the bullshitter draw us in? By creating an air of reasonableness, by presenting some established well-known accuracy to start their bullshit. Bullshitters are masters of implication, and by implication, if they start with well-known established reality, this is what they will seem to continue to do.

But they will gradually progress away from actual truths, to the unsupported lies they're selling, all the while asserting their nonsense with that same reasonable certainty, continually pushing the idea that what they're saying is sensible and true. A crafty tricky illusion, which relies on our inattention and often, our willingness and desire to believe.

Wanting to Believe

"If the motivation behind the 'story' is awareness, growth, and learning to live more consciously, the stories provide fuel, direction, insight. However, some stories are just for facade, for image, for illusion, and just foster the capacity for some to be phenomenally delusional in their grandiose pomposity."

Our complicity is further leveraged because typically such bullshit taps into what we *want* to believe. We're tricked by the appeal to our egos, by making us feel cool because we're part of something, (the bullshit) feeling smart because our theories and beliefs are being "proven," and similar such mechanisms which suck us in by manipulating our egos and our desperations by leveraging our wants and desires. A great example of this are the multitude of conspiracy videos out there.

Conspiracy bullshit employs this format consistently, as does the bullshitter when trying to suck us into the conspiracy of believing they're more than they really are.

The delusion of the bullshitter is dependent on all its component parts. If one aspect collapses with proven certainty, the entire false edifice implodes. They know this, hence their unrelenting insistence on forcing their bullshit. Once we recognise their basic bullshit formulas, the rubbish becomes easy to spot. Mostly we simply have to pose the question, "What am I being *asked* to believe?"

"Real self-improvement requires self-honesty and self-acceptance. Emulating someone else just for the appearance of self-improvement is delusional pompous preening. Vanity is easy to do, no thinking required! Its very obviousness is its appeal. Real self-improvement entails complexity."

The complexity of their bullshit delusion, a delusion they really want to believe, and the ever-increasing fragility of their false reality, leads the bullshitter to a kind of paranoia. They become hyper-concerned with every potential implication, every possible threat, which could pop their ever-thinning expanding bubble of delusion. A bubble they have to keep feeding, a bubble of ever-desperate desperation. The insecurity of untruth, of perpetual lie, is an intense insecurity, a disease of desperation leading to a disease of deception. An all-consuming deception which envelops them completely. The delusion of bullshit is a deceptive path, leading the bullshitter ever deeper into the darkness of self-destruction.

Unfortunately, if we're not careful, if we don't take care, if we aren't pro-active, if we refuse to believe this cancer is real, we can all too easily be part of the very real negative consequences of bullshit.

"How can we ignore bullshit? Bullshit isn't solitary, as its very purpose is to involve others in deception."

Ch9 - Ego-BS

Being "Special"

"There's nothing as ridiculous, as preposterous, as absurd, as dangerous as self-importance run amuck."

Ego is a fictional idea, centred around the belief we need to be special in some way, that we need the approval, attention, and good opinion of others. Ego's principal corruption stems from its main flaw, that we only need the *appearance* of some sort of specialness. That we only need to "look" a certain way to promote ourselves and thereby "stand out" and in some way gain value. For the ego, value is intimately associated with approval, praise, and other such hollow mechanisms. The image, not actual real value, is what matters. Ego is especially preoccupied with the belief it *has* to be special in some way. If it isn't, it "has" to be unhappy. Ego isn't the all of us, fortunately. But for those who become consumed by ego, it becomes their world, resulting in a severe distortion of perspective.

Ego is a logic based on primitive animalistic pressures, when procreation and other benefits *were* intimately connected to appearance, looks, and other superficial characteristics. In today's world, there's much more to life, many ways to be happy. We no longer need ego. What matters in life, what makes a difference, is good character, sensibility, goodness-of-being, self-improvement efforts, and much more which isn't ego.

"Ego is a grand liar."

The BMN is totally taken in by ego logic. Real underlying value is of little interest unless it can promote the pressing agenda of approval, attention, admiration, and praise generation. That's what it's all about, some kind of specialness. The focus here is their intimate understanding of ego, how they use this knowing to try and manipulate us, using our bits of ego bullshit to influence and affect us, trapping us with our own nonsense.

When it comes to ego, the BMN is obsessive, understanding it intimately, using even small amounts in others to exploit them. The simple ego issue of not wanting to cause a "scene" or unpleasantness of any kind, for instance, is regularly taken advantage of. Paying attention to how our own egos are perhaps leveraged alerts us and prevents us from being manipulated.

Just to be clear, there are positive aspects to ego. We're simply focused on the detrimental to aid our understanding. Sadly, when it comes to the BMN, they're not nice people. There's little or nothing redeeming about them, their entire persona is false, predicated on false goals and motivations. Promotion of their ego being a constant and continuous preoccupation and obsession, rendering them incapable of genuine interactions.

One-Sided

"Bullshit-manipulator-narcissists cannot bear to forgo their parasitic entanglements as the absence of this energy-feed leads to major ego-approval withdrawals."

Entanglement is a powerful mechanism used to foster ego-boosting. Usually this is accomplished via the simple mechanism of "friendship" and being "friendly." Under the normal rules of interaction, friends take an interest in each other's activities, listen to each other, support each other, and so on. The key ingredient is *each other*. Reciprocation. For the BMN this is a totally one-sided deal. They may make token appeasements or phoney gestures to appear as if they're providing some value, but really it's all about them.

They abuse the goodness of their "friends" with this one-sidedness, who naturally don't last very long. Here it is they exploit one's own ego especially. They will appeal to us, seemingly, for "advice" or help of some kind, making us feel valuable or important, but it's simply a trick to exploit our time and energy, our egos. They're always involved to "get" something, to build "connections," or some such. If we but examine our own motivations for interacting, much quickly becomes apparent.

One-Up

"The arrogance of ego's imagined prowess at bullshit is astonishing. Ego arrogantly tries to make itself believe when it's able to bullshit others, it's smarter. Hence putting one over someone is such a sought-after ego triumph."

The downside to interacting with this level of

bullshit is that no matter what one says or does, *always* there's this continuous attempt to "top it," or to assert some sort of superiority. Often fault will be found where there's none, or alternative and utterly ridiculous suggestions are made with the only purpose to somehow suggest they're "better."

A tiresome mind-suck of inanity. Their ego fixation simply cannot bear to give credit or acknowledge value if it doesn't in some way reflect back on them. When one is selecting team members, it's particularly helpful to pay attention to this aspect of being.

Ganging-Up

"The root of the us-against-you distortion is an attempt to subvert the accuracy and honesty which isn't in alignment with the short-cut fantastical ego delusion."

When the ego-obsessed mindset encounters those with whom they can't feel some sort of superiority, they resort to war. They utterly resent those who, in their silly view, are "better" than them. It's worthwhile looking out for this toxic, poisonous, and corrosive presence, as this mindset won't think twice of resorting to sabotage to assert some kind of relative one-upmanship.

One tactic they're fond of, when they feel out-classed, is to "gang-up." They'll find others, whether they're in general agreement or not, and ensnare them in an us vs them interaction. The BMN will use their proxy to confront where they're unable to, making every effort to get their accomplice, willing or not, to put the person who they can't themselves deal with "in their place." This tactic is a bullshit cheat, an attempt at accomplishing what they themselves are unable to.

This inevitably happens when their bullshit is called, and some measure of patience and deliberation is applied, preventing them from squirming out of the truth, an eventuality most aggrieving to them. They just can't let a "loss" go. It burns and rankles and sticks with them, until they find a way to secure some kind of "win" over what they now regard as their opponent. It doesn't matter in the least that the "win" is in something completely unrelated to the original incident.

"Some people would rather continue to be fooled than admit that they have been, or are, being fooled."

It's astonishing how the bullshitter can "erase" the awful truth of the initial incident with some bogus manufactured "win." Such is the logic of bullshit and how this mindset manipulates itself to avoid what's intolerable to them, usually, "looking bad" or being wrong in some way. It's such a huge deal to them that they will devote all they have in attempting to remedy these unacceptable occurrences.

They will go to such extremes that they will compromise and self-sabotage themselves, even unto ruin, all to secure that ego victory. One more instance of the preposterousness of this psychology, and how it gets caught up in immersion bubbles, where the limited truths, beliefs, and perceptions within that bubble are all that apply. Yes, it most certainly is a form of madness and mental compromise, as it represents a substantial distortion of reality.

Justifying Crappiness

"Scripting and manipulating information about one's feelings to maintain an image facade only leads to further turmoil and more inner conflict."

Ego-boosting and narcissism are part of the Hollywood-Madison Avenue culture, who use it as a manipulation sales tool. They deliberately legitimise crappiness, justify it, and make their potential customers happy because they're being told they're wonderful, just as they already are.

By association, they love what's being sold. This "sell" is a massively insidious problem. It has led to a societal narcissism and unsubstantiated over-belief in self. The short-term shallow benefits are seemingly great, but has led to a mass bullshit mindset.

This justification of crappiness does exactly what the bullshitter practises, using bullshit logic to cover up the truth. Even worse, because this nonsense is coming at us in ways which are subtle, ways which are assimilated without conscious thought, they change fundamental beliefs and values.

The root of the issue: indulgence! A quality of being not-good, but it has come to be sold as being okay, no problem, The "just-be-you," and "you're okay just as you are" bullshit logics, which have been, and are constantly being pushed, have lulled many into a totally false sense of self. That same false sense of self the bullshitter has.

"Ego is a total idiot."

No, it's *not* okay to just vent your anger or irritation whenever it comes. No, it's *not* okay to be rude, belittling, demeaning, and derogatory to whoever and whenever, just because they happen to have the temerity to disagree with *you*. This culture of legitimising indulgence is directly responsible for the negativity and un-civility culture online. Those who spread their pus online do so because they feel they can.

It's not just because they can get away with it, the problem lies in them feeling they *want* to be horrid in the first place. It's their belief that it's okay to "just be you." The massive problem is when that you is mean, nasty, narcissistic, and bent on dominance and superiority, and believes it has to pull others down to get relative status, the result is those internet and other bullies.

"The bullshitter's entire psychology is maintained by the lie of benefit in the face of repeated non-benefit."

Our own egos can be powerful weapons used against us. Used to manipulate us into crappiness, all for the sake of profit or the ability to manipulate our emotions. Once we become addicted to ego-boosting and to being made to feel good about our crappiness, we're lost. We fall into the blackhole of bullshit. The longer-term problem with this cultivated false belief of self is that over time, as the truth of reality knocks down those false beliefs, we come to realise this untruth we've created.

Sadly, many now face the awful truth, that they've allowed themselves to be tricked into acting like a fool, and this is a painful and awkward truth they don't even want to face, let alone acknowledge or have it be seen and known by others, thus becoming trapped, and can't change. Again, they get caught by their ego. They know that their "looking good" was all false, but now they don't want to "look bad" either. So they get caught by the ego's deception. Swept away by the tsunami of dishonesty they've created within. All because they sold out to the bullshit constantly being pushed at them to be a bullshitter and a narcissist themselves.

"Bullshit will consume us utterly if we allow it."

This is the cancer of bullshit. A pervasive force masquerading as benign. A negativity eating away at us from the inside, but one our defences don't recognise as a threat. So it eats and eats, and corrupts and corrupts our internal selves, hollowing us out from within.

Bullshit is most absolutely not something minor; it's a *huge* problem, one that destroys many, and is a severe infection of our society. Bullshit is a cancer that can only be treated by understanding that it's a cancer, by developing an awareness and an insight into what constitutes deception and how it works. Once we recognise this cancer, we can eradicate the disease of bullshit.

"Gross ego obsession is so utterly pathetic, yet, a reality."

The negative focus we're forced to use with some of our writing in this work bothers us somewhat. Our aim with this book is an unwinding of immersion into beliefs, perspectives, attitudes, and perceptions which prevent personal progression and are limiting. One of those is not seeing, and thus not actually believing, in the existence of certain negativities in the larger world. Especially when those negativities are an extension, exaggeration, and variation of ourselves.

When the utterly pathetic is focused on and pointed out, and its reality is acknowledged, it allows for an awareness of that smaller measure within the self. It's precisely our aim to point out the extreme, because most good people, no matter how self-deprecating or how much they think they need to improve, won't truthfully describe themselves as *utterly* pathetic. So that quote is powerful for enabling a perspective of relative perception. A perception which enables the awareness of what we might not otherwise see or believe exists. When it comes to the negativity of some others, this can be extremely detrimental and dangerous.

Many don't want to engage in self-improvement because they feel overwhelmed by the enormity of the task. When seeing that they're not really as bad as they think, and what they thought was them is in fact not so, there's a change of self-belief. When we believe we aren't as bad as we thought and thus not hopeless, engaging in active self-development becomes a viable proposition.

Thus, in that one little quote, lies much.

Ch10 - The Myth-of-Agreement

Idiotic Agreements

"Why this 'forcing of sanctioning?' - Because they KNOW their agendas and motivations are askew! They themselves don't agree with their own doings and are looking for absolution of responsibility! They don't want to take a stand, so they foist it on others to avoid responsibility by petitioning and manipulating others to 'agree.' Agreement, they believe, makes them 'right.' This is a shortcut to avoiding responsibility! This is how bullshit-manipulators self-justify and self-delude!"

"If I'm not in it alone, I'm not guilty." Bullshitters con themselves with beliefs like this. If they can get in agreement with others, that makes things okay, or so they want to believe. Mostly, it's about getting others in agreement with them, because they want to satisfy their indulgences. Right and wrong is determined by who agrees with whatever they want to do. This myth-of-agreement is hard for good people to understand, especially the implication that good and bad are entirely flexible, that ethics and standards are adjusted as convenient.

Avoiding Accountability

"Those who are lazy about their personal beliefs, and perhaps choose to hold beliefs they know are askew and are just plain indulgent also want their beliefs sanctioned, even though uncool. Hence, they're easily manipulated by bullshit-manipulators! One reveals the other... associations have their implications."

Avoiding responsibility is a huge goal and motivation behind much the bullshitter does. If they're responsible, then they can be held accountable, an eventuality they avoid at all costs. Everything with them is a lie, accountability is linked to exposure, their big fear.

They like to spread the risk, and like to associate with those who also like doing this. They can reinforce each other. Not just in spreading risk, but in mutually supporting indulgences, desired beliefs, and thinking. An old saying appropriately adapted to apply to this bullshit arrangement of convenience: "Birds of a feather lie together."

Inadvertent Condoning

"Bullshitter-manipulators bank on folks not wanting to make the extra effort required to deal with the uncomfortable and awkward truths. And that's how folks get manipulated and duped, and are complicit to the

egregious acts of bullshitters. Condoning bullshit, however subtle, isn't an option! Complicity isn't an option!"

We can agree without agreeing, by not disagreeing. Yes, it seems tricky at first, but our lack of disagreement is *taken* by the bullshitter as agreement. They will act and behave *as if* we agreed. A clever manipulative trick. Or at least they like to think so. They leverage our dislike and avoidance of confrontation, awkwardness, and un-comfortableness to pressure us with our own crappiness into "letting it be."

We think we're choosing the lesser of the evils, but we're not. Letting cancer alone when it starts, is a severe action with severe consequences. We can't allow bullshit to be condoned, no matter how inadvertently. We become responsible for what it leads to. Seldom does it matter in the immediate, but always it matters in the long-term.

Crappy Conscience

"Bullshitters will go to great lengths to manipulate and force a public perception of agreement in an attempt to assuage a guilty conscience and dented ego."

This manipulation of their own conscience is a fascinating self-bullshit. Why does it work for the bullshitter? Because they're hollow inside. Because their lives are made of figment and not real learning and growing, not acquiring a real and independent self, they're hollow. They take on whatever is the prevailing "should." They adapt to whatever they think is currently "cool" or "in," and whatever they believe will get them approval and attention.

That's their focus. All that matters is that "they," most in their circle or community, or even people in general, believe and feel whatever the bullshitter has taken on as their own. These deceivers are ethical chameleons, chameleons of conscience. Whatever works, whatever is convenient. They're chameleons with a special trick: They change the environment to suit the colour they want to show. When that colour is the colour of an erased conscience, they will go to great lengths to manufacture agreement from enough to allow them to apply their myth-of-agreement. "If enough agree, then it's okay."

"Overriding conscience is a slow suicide of self. Conscience cannot be absolved with bullshit."

One would think bullshitters and especially BMNs, don't have a conscience, but they do. It's exactly because they do have some bit of conscience that they resort to lies. Deception is the cover-up, the obfuscation, they need to hide themselves from their conscience. It's this that makes bullshitters so terrible. They *know* what they do is wrong. Yet they do it anyway.

They transgress against themselves because they absolutely insist on their indulgences. They refuse to give these up, believing that doing so makes them "losers" and "inferior." So thoroughly enslaved are they by their root mis-beliefs, it causes them to go against themselves, resulting in perpetual misery and no hope of actual happiness, leaving them to resort to bullshit happiness.

Ethical Emptiness

"The mis-belief that agreement equates rightness cannot be used to manipulate the absolution of corrupt conscience. The root belief of the conformity mindset is that 'if others do it, it must be okay,' and thus it's a validation, is a myth. Both goodness and crappiness need

to be determined on their own merits. Else we end up with the lowest common denominator."

The crime of bullshit in general, the cancer of bullshit, lies in this constant pulling down of everything. Lower and lower, until we're all in the shitpile with the bullshitter, until we're all lower than them, until there are no standards, no ethics. Until we're at that level of emptiness and indulgence where the bullshitter resides and where they're comfortable. Indulgence constantly drags us down into a place where responsibility and ethics, standards and values, and anything which requires some measure of effort that's not indulging infantile desires doesn't exist.

When we understand that the bullshitter psychology hasn't matured past that childish stage of wanting whatever it wants no matter what, then much becomes clear. They've learned that much of what they want is *not* okay, but they've also learned they can manipulate their wants and desires into being okay, if they can get others to agree with them. Bullshitters love the myth-of-agreement, as it enables them.

Corrupting Justification

"Legitimacy and validation, when not inherently determined by criteria such as ethics, logic, and reason, are then 'proven' by alternate means such as like-minded agreement and association, which are subtly leveraged to validate, pushing the notion that when others believe it, it must be true. If others validate it, it must be so. It's a deception of mutually reinforcing personal dishonesty."

The usefulness of the myth-of-agreement works both ways. Those they involve also benefit from this usefulness. Often these are actually good people, but ones that for whatever reason become fixed on a particular agenda that's important to them. Sadly, they will compromise their goodness and their ethics to achieve their agenda, justifying these transgressions of conscience with that insidious distortion: "The end justifies the means."

Unfortunately, this belief just helps spread corruption and inevitably leads to a stained result, not to mention the complications and problems now caused by those "means." Solving one problem at the cost of creating others is no solution at all. Polluting the world to clean up an island is hardly beneficial. Good people often succumb to bullshit logic when they become immersed in some focus or other they believe in. Whenever we compromise our ethics, we enter into bullshit, a slippery slope, which only leads to the shitpile.

"There's a group dynamic at play which is insidious, corrupt, and subtle when the implied consent and validation of bullshit are willingly bought into."

Good people are also vulnerable to the myth-of-agreement. They very much can fall prey to this belief that "if everybody thinks it's good, it is." All manner of horrors in history have been perpetrated in the name of this myth. The idea that agreement constitutes rightness or goodness is just bullshit. If we look at superstitions we quickly see the lie and nonsense of this belief.

Vacuous Validity

"Implied agreement and approval fosters the notion of validity when there's none. 'If others agree with me, I must be right.'"

The difficulty with this particular bullshit belief is

that when it comes to determining truth, rightness, and goodness, we're really on our own. A responsibility few are willing to undertake. Lest we're also prepared to be bullshitters, however limited, we have to be willing to stand alone when it comes to the responsibilities of being a good and decent person.

We have to make those hard decisions for ourselves. Right or wrong, *we* have to make the choice, *we* have to take the responsibility, and we simply have to do our best. It's all we can do. We have help, we only have to look at the bullshitter and see their miserable hollow corrupt lives and selves to warn us of the dangers and detriments of not being our own person. The bullshitter is utterly corrupted because of their refusal to be a real person.

"Joiners, followers, and 'fans' who also have compromised ways, beliefs, and agendas are simply, by association, deemed to validate wilful indulgences, and thus mutually reinforce a lack of ethics. The soliciting of what are really accomplices is an attempt to legitimise unsubstantiated attitudes, behaviours, and beliefs."

If we look at bullshitters who have a "following," who have admirers and sycophants, we see a sad group. Toadies and spineless panderers who have nothing are nothing, who are desperate for any crumb. A thoroughly odious situation. When looking at this from the outside, we clearly see its corruption, and how we want nothing at all to do with such a crowd, and the idea of being part of it is beyond horrible.

We have to consider that whenever we bullshit, even in small ways, ways we think are insignificant, we're in fact joining such a group, a group that pollutes the world. Just because we're not clearly in a particular circle doesn't mean we're not in a larger less well defined association. If we bullshit ourselves, even a little, we join that greater gang of defilement.

If we care about our world, how, just how, do we justify polluting it with bullshit?

Ch11 - Co-opting Complicity

Leveraging Social Awkwardness

"Bullshit-manipulator-narcissists turn indulgence into a way-of-being! Public agreement or condonance of indulging is a slippery slope. This is how allegiance gets co-opted, how bullshit entanglements and groupings come into being: by co-opting the goodness of generally good people and turning it into complicity."

Indulging their desire to be seen as "nice" and "friendly" and "cool" is of vital importance to the BMN. They're acutely aware of all the nuance involved with this indulgence. So intimately acquainted are they with all the ins and outs of appearance, image, and the approval-disapproval of others that they're able to use and manipulate this knowing innately. They will fully exploit the desire of good people to not cause unpleasantness, to not be rude, to not make a scene and to not "look bad." These are *our* indulgences. Yes, to a greatly lesser degree, but the BMN will exploit and use them without qualm.

Our desire to be Good, and to thus give the benefit of the doubt, to trust, to not think ill of others, to not be unpleasant, and similar, are all turned on us. If we're wimpy and "weak," refusing to stand up for ourselves or to call BS when it's egregious or otherwise fail to do what's right, despite being unpleasant, we only have ourselves to blame if our indulgence is used against us. The worst of it is we become *complicit* in the unethical doings of the BMN.

"Bullshit cannot survive on its own. It requires complicity of some sort."

For instance, you and your partner are in a group social setting with a BMN whom you both know, but the rest of those present do not. Someone mentions a need for assistance of some kind. The BMN pipes up and presents a bullshit picture of how they can be of help. You and your partner know this is rubbish, but saying something will severely embarrass your BMN "friend" or could cause an argument and a "scene." So you keep silent and let it run its course.

The BMN knows you're likely to not say anything, and your lack of opposition or disagreement will be used by them, through subtle implication to lend support to their bullshit self-promotion. The person on the receiving end who has no way of knowing thus believes the BMN, as there's no reason not to. They take your non-opposition as agreement or support for the BMN and their claims. It's all innocent on the surface. The person asking for assistance has no idea of what's really going on and will only find out later, when it's too late.

"There's no goodness in appeasement, as it's

simply inappropriate tolerance. A mis-belief we cannot afford."

Problem is, we're now *complicit* in embroiling that person with the bullshit of the BMN. Unfortunately, BMNs always overestimate their abilities, biting off way past realistic ambitions. They like the image, status, and *appearance* of being capable even beyond what their bullshit promises, but can seldom deliver. Always, when failing to live up to their hype, they use bullshit to get them out of trouble, blaming everything else but themselves.

Nonetheless, the person at the receiving end has had their time or money wasted. The worst part of this is that we're entirely complicit through our non-action. The sooner we realise we can't always just say nothing to avoid potential unpleasantness, the sooner we enable ourselves to act. Because our goodness will also not allow us to be complicit. We simply need to realise and become aware of this consequence. As good people, it then becomes our e*thical* duty to not be complicit!

Implied Endorsement

"The manipulation of my consent and positive interaction is being forced from me, and this is just wrong! Bad! This forcing of my positivity is to sanction the bullshit-manipulator's being, which is actually sanctioning their manipulation, their crappiness, their lack of ethics and integrity. This is stealing my goodness, impinging on my positivity! This is how bullshit-manipulator-narcissists steal freedom! 'I accept and respect your difference; just don't force and manipulate me into sanctioning it!' We were never friends, so the agenda to be 'friends' and appear 'friendly' is suspect! The coercion of my positive interaction for wrong-motivation is totally unethical!"

BMNs cross the lines of normal polite interaction. They will engineer forced agreements through casual innocuous seeming remarks like: "I'm sure you'll all agree." Or using someone's name deliberately, as in: "I'm sure Joe will agree," then smoothly moving on. This co-opted support is gained in passing and never focused on directly. The bullshitter directs attention via emphasis elsewhere, obscuring that tacit endorsement, making it difficult for us to not go along with this subtle manipulation and thereby securing that all-important implied substantiation.

What they're asking agreement to is usually so undefined, it's hard to object. Likewise, they will use our general goodness to, by implication, support them. They can assume a "friendship" based on nothing more than our positivity and friendliness. Overstepping the boundaries of normal polite interaction to force an implied sanctioning of their bullshit, and thus by implication, of their being and their agendas, as their bullshit is usually some sort of self-promotion.

It's a sneaky trick, because how do we object? If we say, "Hey, we aren't friends yet, I haven't gone that far," then we're the ones who seem petty and ridiculous. Likely the BMN will just turn around and say something like, "What makes you think we are? That's a bit presumptuous," thus turning the tables on us.

The only way to deal with this is to learn to recognise the bullshitters and BMNs, and through being aware, forestall such actions by withholding our positivity and friendliness until we're sure they won't be abused and misused. All we really need is merely to withhold for even a few seconds, to simply not make our perceptions and interactions with others automatic. Once our positivity, and thus our implied approval is given, it's difficult to take back.

A particular solution to the above example, when the bullshitter claims agreement on our behalf, would be a simple polite shake of the head or a neutral, "Um, no." Just this is enough to direct emphasis on their ploy, collapsing all their trickery and bullshit. The implications of our simple action are immediately apparent. The bullshitter now knows we know, making us dangerous to use as a forced ally. Once is usually enough, as the bullshitter is careful to not risk exposure. A chance they never take unless they absolutely have to.

Once they know we see their game and won't play along, they will look elsewhere for unaware allies to co-opt. If the Joe isn't us and doesn't notice or is unaware of their inadvertent complicity, we can still derail the bullshit with something like "Do you, Joe?"

Simple non-acceptance and non-agreement derails inadvertent complicity; going a long way towards thwarting manipulated entanglement into bullshit.

Forced Friendliness

"Bullshit-manipulators coerce our politeness, sneakily embroiling us in a non-existent relationship or agreement. It's about forcing an interaction! Being aware of this manipulation is key."

As Murphy stated in one of his other laws, "It's easier to get into things than to get out." We get tricked by the *seeming* friendliness and charm of the BMN. If we take those extra few seconds to look deeper, to ask, "What's the intent here?" we usually get a clue that something isn't as it seems. This pause is all we need to prevent interacting in ways that will lead us astray.

For good people, this isn't easy, as we wish for everyone

to be good and nice. We wish there are no bad people, we wish for goodness and positivity. In the real world, awareness is the issue. We *can* be good, and nice, and positive, *AND* aware, all at the same time. We simply need to build that pause and that discernment into our habitual interactions and behaviours.

"Bullshit-manipulator-narcissists are insistent on getting their foot in the door! Any door! Just saying hello or hi can be a manipulation of our goodness. This hi-jacking of our goodness is a segway into a relationship that one doesn't necessarily want to be part of."

It's not easy to respond to known BMNs when we meet them out in the world. They will greet us with a great friendliness like we're long-time close friends. Especially if we've come to know what exactly they are, and we know they're not nice and good people. Our instinct and habit is to respond to friendliness with friendliness.

But with a known BMN we need to check that impulse, responding with neutrality instead. Responding with an awareness that transmits, "I know what you are and want no part of it, thanks." Typically, bullshitters fear awareness. It's their Kryptonite. Awareness of bullshit reflects what's going on, and bullshit can't thrive when it's obviously bullshit; then it's just lame.

"We like to believe that our non-specific actions don't make us complicit, but they do! We're just as accountable for our non-actions as our actions. Inadvertent complicity through irresponsible inattention and inaction has unfavourable consequences not readily apparent. We tend to believe that complicity is only an overt and deliberate action, but this isn't the case."

Non-action is a powerful lever for the bullshitter. If we don't object or express overt disagreement, we're deemed to agree. We're thus automatically made complicit. The leverage used is that we don't want to go around being disagreeable.

There are many ways to disagree without actually saying anything, and these are the most powerful when dealing with bullshit. We merely have to *show* that we don't agree, we don't have to spell it out or say why. For many this might be difficult, but if we don't, we become complicit, allowing bullshitters to get away with their bullshit.

Too Much Effort

"The willingness of good folks to be deceived because of their reluctance to think things through, their desire for a quick and easy answer, and to place responsibility on someone else and avoid the stresses of independent thinking makes them complicit. Their willingness to believe confidence leads them deeply astray. Confidence is not enough."

Complicity comes in many forms. Our laziness, our reluctance to take a stand, our unwillingness to "get involved," our resistance to thinking about things, to deal with a "heavy" topic, and our dislike of dealing with unpleasant truths all make us complicit. We like to think we avoid involving ourselves with the unpleasant and the bad, but that avoidance is exactly what makes us complicit, because we allow it to exist, to continue, to carry on.

If we think of bullshit as a virus, as an infectious disease, it changes matters considerably. Especially when it comes to the BMN. Their narcissism takes non-resistance as agreement, thus they take our non-action as condoning them. A severely dangerous and potentially disastrous path we're part of putting them on.

Bullshit is the start. Unchecked and affirmed delusion enables all their rotten tendencies and can lead to severely bad and criminal behaviour, especially once they start to feel invulnerable.

"It takes less energy and is simpler and quicker to indulge and appease bullshit than to confront or deal with it. There's a social convention to placate, appease, and condone bullshit to facilitate 'pleasant' interaction."

If we but think things through a bit when it comes to bullshit, we quickly see it's not a simple issue, not a nothing issue, but a serious problem hidden in the seemingly non-serious, innocuous, and trivial. Pretence hides all sorts of ills, and this is what makes it so dangerous, especially because it's through this disguise that our complicity is stolen. Much like cancer grows because it fools our immune system, so bullshit eats at goodness.

Mass Mis-Beliefs

"The externally-influenced-persona, the bullshitter-narcissist, is predicated on the false premise that communally supported behaviour is valid, but it's not, because much behaviour is typically only supported to avoid conflict."

The bullshitter likes convenient beliefs such as: "But if everyone does it, it must be okay" or, "If everyone agrees, it must be right." Both of these are false. We can look at history and superstitions to see how false they are. These beliefs are how our complicity is hijacked.

If we're taken to be in agreement because we say nothing, because we don't object or disagree, we're one of those masses that makes that false belief seem true and valid.

We become part of the problem, part of the mis-belief. We're complicit.

It's exactly this which allows bad politicians and other societal ills to exist. It's a particular problem when it comes to bullshitters, because they're fully aware of this mechanism and actively use it to further their bullshit by obtaining a seeming overall general agreement, and thus, their bullshit comes to be taken as true, simply because no one had the gumption, courage, nor ethics to object and disagree. They know most people don't like to go against the crowd, no matter how true and obvious the truth might be.

"If you're willing to believe whatever suits your purpose without substantiation or validation, you deserve to be manipulated."

Just so. If we do nothing, we're complicit. And responsible.

Ch12 - Dealing with Inconvenience

"'Big Jim' did not bring much to the discussions during meetings, but he was very good at stopping bullshit with his disapproving look."

Unpleasant Truth

"I have found, when we make the effort to answer the odd and peculiar, sometimes inconvenient questions, which we cannot avoid if we're honest, we come to that point where we can actually translate them into utilisable awareness."

Most often that question is as simple as, "What's going on?" We often ask this question, but just leave it there. It's an expression and acknowledgement by us that something isn't exactly right. Typically, we don't look deeper.

If we go further and actually work out and think about what's really going on, we get to see the fullness of the situation. This might not be convenient or pretty. It's better to know beforehand when there's still opportunity to deal with matters than leaving it to fester and complicate, and eventually cause us much more hassle and trouble.

"Indulgent cringe-fests and untrustworthy experiences allow one to act on that awareness if we pay attention and learn. Awareness brings with it accountability. Awareness without application is meaningless."

A powerful quote which has much to it. If we're cringing or embarrassed or uncomfortable or in any way put out by someone's behaviour or words, it's a clear warning. If we, as most people do, cover this up, refuse to pay attention, and otherwise hide from awkwardness, we only enable the bullshitter, especially when they aim to manipulate us.

They count on our aversion to unpleasantness and deliberately create situations that leverage our reluctance to deal with the awkward and uncomfortable. They know they can say and do all manner of outrageousness, and we won't object or call them out because we're afraid of unpleasantness or simply don't want to be inconvenienced.

That supposed convenience is a massive price to pay for the entanglement and complicity through this support of the bullshit. If we don't show in some way that we're not in support, bullshitters will use our silence, evasion, and non-objection as agreement. They will do this actively.

Unfortunately there are times we just have to bite the bullet, suck it up, and deal with that inconvenience, awkwardness, and unpleasantness. Even sometimes initiating it. If we don't, we will forever thereafter be held hostage by our wimpiness and weakness. We don't have to make a scene or do anything drastic. We merely need to let our position be known.

We can do this quietly, softly, without fuss. Often we can show where we're at simply with our awareness, posture, or expression. A disapproving look seen by all can stop a bullshitter most effectively. We merely have to have just that bit of courage, decency, and ethics to not allow the infection of bullshit to spread. Bullshit is a disease of negativity, no matter how much it may be disguised in apparent "friendliness" and other supposed positive disguises. It's *not* cool, or nice, or harmless. Quite the opposite.

"It takes all sorts to make up the ecosystem. Rotten apples belong in the compost - it's inappropriate to have them at your dinner table."

Acknowledging Ignorance

"The acknowledgement of ignorance is a necessity - it's part of life. Without this simple acceptance, learning is near impossible."

An inconvenient truth the bullshitter avoids with all of their being is the acknowledgement of their own ignorance and nincompoopery. It's something we all have, no matter how much we may think otherwise. This is simply a truth. Most of us know this and accept it as part of being human, making efforts to deal with this reality, learning and growing, and in this way improving ourselves.

The bullshitter absolutely refuses to deal with their ignorance and foolishness. A reality that's a horror to them, to be avoided at all costs. They refuse to apply the necessary efforts most people make to remedy this state of affairs. It's their refusal and avoidance of this fact of existence that leads them to resort to bullshit. They use deception to not only cover the truth of what they are, but also use their delusion as a substitute for learning, in the process bullshitting themselves that they're growing.

This is an impossibility. An inconvenient truth they in turn also refuse to face, and thereby create a life which has no hope really. They remain forever ignorant and incompetent, foolish and silly. They can't really ever be anything, as their entire being is founded on this idiotic idea that they can cheat their way into being something. They believe that simply being able to fool others is enough.

It isn't, and the most inconvenient of all the truths is that they can never fool themselves, no matter how hard they try. In the end they always know the real truth about themselves, that they're an empty nothing. What a price to pay, all for the "benefit" of avoiding a simple truth of existence that applies to us all. Sad.

"The mere acquisition of information is neither learning nor intelligence."

The inconvenience of learning doesn't appeal to the bullshitter in the least. Neither does the inconvenience of not being super smart. Instead of making real efforts to deal with these truths, they want to cheat their way to simulating some sort of appearance of intelligence and learning. One of the ways they do this is through repeating and regurgitating information they've picked up.

In particular, bullshitters will repeat and "re-sell" what's impressed *them*. So arrogant and ego-centric are they, that they just assume if *they* didn't know, then no one else did either. They will then take this newfound knowledge and use it to try to impress others, assuming everyone else would be equally impressed. They don't realise just how ignorant they are relative to others, due to their life of lying to themselves about how much they know.

It's an inconvenient reality that their very efforts to try to appear knowledgeable and intelligent are completely counterproductive, aggravating the very reality they're trying to cover up. Even more fascinating is how they will grab onto something someone said, and if it came out impressively and sounded intelligent or wise, or in some way important, they will simply steal, copy, and repeat what they heard without actually even understanding what they're saying. Often they will use this borrowed information and words in a context that's wholly inappropriate, exposing their utter ignorance, foolishness, stupidity, and bullshit.

Usually though, those who know what has happened simply file the implications away, making the appropriate reassessment of the counterfeiter. So caught up is the bullshitter in the *idea* that they're "selling" themselves as clever or wise etc., that they don't realise the counterproductive implications of this ridiculous form of deceit. If it wasn't so tragic, it would be hilarious, and often is.

"The preposterous can happen, does happen, has happened, is happening!"

Implications

"We can't only focus on convenient truths; we have to pay equal attention to the inconvenient."

Our own nonsense, however small, has massive consequences when interacting with bullshitters. Especially our dislike of inconvenient truths. They will exploit this reluctance to deal with those inconvenient, but true, unpleasant realities by leveraging our unwillingness to call them on their rubbish. Or they will manipulate us, knowing we avoid confrontation. There are many ways our own foolishness causes us trouble. BMNs will use whatever they can to further their agendas.

What prevents us from dealing with manipulators appropriately? Usually it's simply our reluctance to make that bit of extra effort. Isn't this short-sightedness of our own, BS of our own? It is. If we wish to deal with bullshit, we have to let go of our own silliness, however small, otherwise the price we pay for that crappiness can be exceedingly high.

Ch13 - Malignant Manipulation

Manipulating Niceness

"The bullshit-manipulator's M.O. is to exploit one's loves and connections, and one's desire to not stress and cause trouble for others. To not cause a scene, to play the game of being friendly, nice, and considerate - everything they're not! Yet purport to be. They care only about their own wants. The entire agenda is to attempt pulling one down to appear better by comparison, and thus feed their narcissism."

The first step in an interaction for a bullshit-manipulator-narcissist is determining their main and almost instinctual objective which is to determine whether their con is working, has worked. If the recipient buys the bullshit, they're dupes and good candidates as "friends," and therefore easily handled, coerced, manipulated, and used for all their resources, connections and reputation.

These "friends" are now "owned" by the BMN and are called upon for help, assistance, and commiseration at every whim to maintain their compliance as serfs to the bullshit-manipulator-narcissist.

Worse Than

"Bullshit-manipulators look to maintain their energetics and entanglements to get their way and piss on a situation, marking it as territory just to justify their being and persona. They'll force the illusion of 'friendliness' or being a good sport. They exploit what's important to others and use that to manipulate and exploit goodness. Anytime one has an attachment to something, it can be exploited. However, if one cares about ethics first and foremost, all other affections are secondary, and it's easy to walk away."

The bullshit-manipulator-narcissist is extremely envious of everybody whom they perceive as "better-than" them. Their psychologies are deeply threatened by simple perceptions like, "wow, here's an actually happy person!" The comparative-mindset of the BMN has to attempt destroying what it believes is critique and unfavourable reflection, even if only by implication.

They will attempt this pull-down with every tactic in their arsenal, starting subtly at first, with passive-aggressive actions, gradually ramping up their efforts if they don't achieve success, eventually ending with full-blown bullying and outright blatant negativity. If possible, they prefer to manipulate their way to some sort of relative "betterness."

This they will do by attempting to establish a form of

control, be it financial, domestic, or social. This dominance can manifest via determining who the other's friends are for them, and what they're "allowed" to do, or other such absurdities. As long as the BMN feels someone is dependent on them in some way, they can bullshit themselves they're "superior."

"The wall-of-energy that bullshitters foist is an emotional, energetic, and psychological entanglement, which is foisted to acquire 'relative status,' by underhanded means, such as: 'better-than,' 'more in-charge,' 'smarter-than,' 'more superior,' 'denigrating,' 'more seductive,' 'invasive,' 'more attractive,' 'demeaning,' 'more hip,' 'derogatory,' 'more cool,' 'dominant,' 'intrusive,' 'ingratiating,' etc. etc. Essentially, an attempt to establish top-dog status or, failing that, implied approval and agreement. Tacit condoning makes you the implied bottom-dog for this type of psychology. And thus relative superiority is finagled."

The bullshit-manipulator-narcissist coerces good people to "open the door" via bullying, allowing them to plunder, take, use, and abuse whatever they will. They're corrupters and polluters of environments. Once they've tainted a situation, a free-for-all is created for other parasites, enabling nefarious dealings and a feeding from their scraps. In the process, glorifying the BMN as benefactors. They enjoy pulling down people and places, relishing corrosion through their indulgence, thus provoking the lowest common denominator in others.

Egregious Association

"The wall-of-energy bullshitters impose exploits lack of disagreement, which is then taken as agreement, even though it's not! The lack of opposition is contorted and manipulated into support, which we're now party to, even

though we don't actually agree!"

The bullshit-manipulator-narcissist needs control and "ownership" of people and things in the guise of being "friends." Maintaining control of the other person and whatever resources they might have by "helping," flattery, solicitations, and seemingly benign "invites." They're infiltrators and polluters of businesses, homes, persons, and communities at large. Association with the BMN has a detrimental impact.

Anyone who's aware and savvy enough to see through the bullshit doesn't want to be associated with nefarious individuals who disguise themselves as "nice" and "friendly." Furthermore, those who do associate with the BMN prove themselves to be fools, and not worth the risk, closing opportunities because of contamination by association.

Pollution cannot happen if doors aren't opened, and folks aren't amenable to bullshit and skewed agendas. Discernment is required regarding who we let into our homes, hearts, and businesses, otherwise we allow ourselves to be manipulated via our simple but naive friendliness.

"The intent-distortion bullshitter's leverage is an emotional, energetic, and psychological entanglement foisted upon others to engineer complicit agreements using overt lack of disagreements. A manipulative bullying which abuses people's goodness, politeness, and courtesy. Why do bullshitters impose this energy around their core of distortion? Because it requires counter-energy to break through the purported 'innocuous' intent and get to the underlying crappiness. It's more expedient in energy expenditure terms to just be herded with the prevailing imposition than it is to resist."

Ch14 - Depths of Discernment

"Oh no! We've slithered into a bullshit zone Ethel. Stare straight ahead, don't make eye contact, do not smile, stay calm and keep on moving!"

Conspirators

"Bullshit is a conspiracy."

We're part of the conspiracy without even fully realising. Or perhaps we do. Whenever we pander to bullshit, whenever we allow it to propagate through our inactions and non-actions, whenever we turn a blind-eye, whenever we smile and nod in response to gross false bullshit, we become part of the conspiracy. A conspiracy we're being asked to condone by implication.

"It's not just what bullshit-manipulators say; it's all in the theatre of their eyes, smile, awareness, attitude, walk, talk, voice, script, laugh, energy, posture, hand gestures, face projection, hair, attire. Etcetera."

Bullshitters also conspire with each other. Not directly, rather subtly, by implication. They feed each other's delusions with mutually reinforcing agreements and the appearance of providing benefit because of their contortions.

For instance, A has something B wants, who schmoozes A to get it, believing as is their habit, "this is the way it's done." A, in this instance, has to supply the benefit anyway. B just happens to be available, and A, also being a bullshitter, seizes on the opportunity to make B think they're giving out the benefit *because* of B's manipulations, making them feel their efforts paid off. A in turn gets the "advantage" of making B beholden to them. Thus they enter their conspiracy of falsehood. Of course the moment neither needs the other, they will drop them immediately. Bullshit conspirators have no loyalty.

Ugly Truths

"We only call it bullshit because we're uncomfortable and awkward dealing with the innate deception and underlying ugliness of these 'non-deliberate' machinations."

Discernment is unfortunately not always pretty nor pleasant. If we're to avoid being inadvertent conspirators in the proliferation of deception which abounds today, we need to deal with that unpleasantness. This doesn't mean we need to confront or "call out" every bullshitter we encounter. We needn't necessarily even deal with *any* of them.

What we do need to face are our inner perceptions. We need to go where our discernment leads us. Not shying away from uncomfortable truths. Yes, the side effect is that we bring the crap of bullshit into our world, but it's better to see the shit and know it's there than step in it.

Deliberate Motives

"Bullshit is more than exaggeration; it's deeper, deliberate, deceitful... An ugly lying because the intent is to deceive!"

In our everyday lives, we encounter bullshit, we know such persons, but typically don't pay it much mind. "It's just nonsense." If we think about it, how did that "nonsense" happen? Randomly? No, unfortunately not. It didn't "just come out."

With some attention, we quickly see there had to be some thought behind that falseness; not the specific words maybe, but the *intent* and the agenda. Why exactly are they putting out what isn't? This is the question to ask. What's the motive behind it? Now we get somewhere. Through this we come to understand that the rubbish isn't idle nor mere happenstance. Deceit, or manipulation, these motivations are ever near. There's an agenda and an intent to present the self as something other than what it is. Deception is lying, usually just indirect lying, but still lying. Manipulation is also oblique lying, and worse, it's abuse.

"Covert arrogance... timid bullying... deceptions which we have to be aware of. Hence the necessity for discernment."

If we ask ourselves, "If I were to bullshit, what would be my purpose? What would be behind it?" Coming at the intent from the other side quickly allows us to see what's involved. Can we simply just push falsehood for no reason? Not likely. Behind the deceptions are real reasons, and those reasons aren't nice.

If we strip away the deception of our own refusal to deal with deceit and see it for what it really is, we see the bad intents and motivations behind the pretence. To willingly and knowingly deceive others for some benefit is not nice. There's nothing benign about this, regardless of how much the bullshitter tries to convince us otherwise.

"Some of the worst bullies hide behind a facade of timidity. A timid bully is still a bully; merely a disguised bully!"

The benefits of squarely facing the unpleasant realities underlying bullshit reside in the awareness we gain, allowing us to discern what's really happening. Further understanding of the deceptions and manipulations lie in the implications. What does it say about someone when they deliberately employ abuse and deceit? Implications when it comes to bullshitters aren't nice in the least.

To deliberately deceive and manipulate others means a rottenness of being, it means bullshitters aren't good people. This they know. It's one of the reasons for the distortions in the first place. Their aim is to hide and cover-up this awful fact. Why they take great pains to present themselves as "friendly," even timid or shy, or some other contrived disguise. Discernment is looking past the surface, past what's presented, looking at what lies behind, at what's really going on.

Arrogance

"Arrogance is often well disguised, covert, and subtle. Yet we tend to believe it only exists in overt form."

A distinguishing aspect of bullshitters is their own

awareness of the not-niceness of what they do. They *know* their actions aren't right, they know they're cheating. They know they're stealing from others, stealing our goodwill and positive energy. If what they get from us is a result of falsehood, it's stealing. Because they so clearly know what they're really doing is unjustifiable, they go to great pains to hide and disguise, obfuscate and distract. A vital necessity of deception.

"Mis-perceiving arrogance for confidence, and confidence for good intention, has devastating consequence."

One of our most dangerous mis-perceptions of a BMN occurs when they can successfully sell their arrogance as confidence. Then, via the confidence they convince us they have good intentions, and are acting in our interest. But this isn't possible for them. Their psychologies simply won't permit true selflessness.

No matter how much their actions may seem directed toward the good of others, at bottom there's *always* some personal agenda which is foremost. It may so happen that others derive great benefit, but this won't be to the BMN's liking, because *they* always need to be the one who benefits the most. The only time they can bear to see others benefit is when they're benefiting much more. Always that comparison and hierarchy is present. When we see apparent benefit from a BMN, it's time to be especially wary.

Strategic Neutrality

"There's absolutely no good reason for involvement, 'friendship,' or the appearance of 'friendliness' with a bullshitter. A modicum of civility is a generosity which might be appropriate if not coerced, as there's no real

interest from them in 'friendship' or relating, other than
the agenda of appearances, self-promotion, and relative
superiority. There's no upside to interacting. All it does is
serve to maintain their image-facade. Life is for living, for
sincerity, for integrity, for realness, for true genuineness.
Faking goodness is moronic!"

Interacting with a known bullshitter, especially a
BMN, can be difficult. A challenge requiring the
application of discernment. If we behave and react
according to our natural inclinations and habits of
goodness, responding with friendliness, all we accomplish
is legitimising the bullshitter. Or worse, we likely will
need to deal with entanglement. We also don't want to be
outright unfriendly or rude, even though it might be
warranted. This goes against our grain. Limiting our
interactions and responses to the bare minimum and
maintaining a completely neutral attitude works well.

Yes, there are times when open unfriendliness might be
called for, if the negative actions of a bullshitter are
blatant and undeniable. This is rare, as they take great
pains to "cover" their doings, never opening themselves to
definitive censure. Always everything with them is
unclear. But, our discernment and understanding allows us
to see exactly what they are, and what they're up to.
"Proving" this in a technical sense is difficult. Thus, if
we're openly hostile we run the risk of the bullshitter
going on the counter-offensive. When we're not present,
they can, and will, distort matters in their favour, using our
open hostility as "proof" the fault lies with us. Typical
bullshit tactics.

Our neutral stance, not friendly and not unfriendly, is
powerful when it comes to bullshitters and BMNs. Much
of their distortion and manipulation depends on
implication. Our lack of friendly response to their typical
forced friendliness is by implication an indictment of
them. We also can't be faulted for any supposed

unreasonable or illogical behaviour. Thus, our neutrality is a powerful non-positive reflection on them, especially if this is done in the company of others. Those who notice will see something is amiss and put two and two together, the very result the bullshitter fears most. Public opinion and approval is vitally important to them. They can't easily attack an unbiased stance, without it being obvious they have an agenda, and without them "looking bad." We can use their own nonsense to deal with them.

Neutrality is a powerful tool in our arsenal when dealing with bullshit. We may believe we need to take a strong stand, and we do. When it comes to dealing with these snakes and fakes, they will use anything which is important to us as a lever for manipulation. Any strong emotion lets them know where they can push our buttons, where they can pressure us, and thus how they can manipulate us. Here we apply our discernment to ourselves. Knowing this tactic and potential weakness, we keep our emotions to ourselves, preventing any openings to be exploited.

Corruption

"You can't uncorrupt your conscience by corrupting the conscience of another."

The logic of the bullshitter is the logic of a cheat. All their bullshit is one giant cheat. Everything they do is in some way an attempt to circumvent truth. One such false logic in particular is the distorted notion that if someone else is worse than you, it makes you okay. What an incredibly moronic notion. One bullshitters adopt wholeheartedly because it's so incredibly convenient for them. They want to deceive their way to happiness, to value, to competence, to being real, to everything. They even try to cheat when it comes to their conscience!

To appease their conscience with their relatively-better-makes-me-okay logic, they will make every effort to corrupt the conscience of another. They will try to enlist you in a joint lie or cheating on something in your presence or, with your knowledge, making you guilty by association.

If you don't object, this will later be used to condemn you and point out you *didn't* object and are therefore guilty as well. Now they "have something on you," and in their logic this makes them "superior." It doesn't matter the relative degree of their transgression compared to yours. They will gloatingly point out you're worse than them because you're also a massive hypocrite, going into how you "pretend" to be good and nice, but really you're "just like them," only worse because you're such a huge hypocrite.

All of this is utter bullshit, but that's what the bullshitter does. Mostly this logic isn't even expressed, but just their internal distortions in this regard are enough to give them belief in their "superiority" and your "inferiority." These mis-beliefs and idiocies will manifest in their demeanour and behaviour, and worse, they will communicate their perverted attitudes of you to others. A problem when associating with bullshitters, especially the BMN, since we *are* guilty, simply through association, regardless of what we do. Merely associating with a bullshitter inadvertently condones their behaviour and actions, and they will use this fact to entangle us in their corrupt convolutions.

Discernment

"Bullshit is its own blackhole. You can't fix bullshit with more."

Bullshitters start with a cheat mindset, a gain-at-the-expense-of-others belief system, with their insistence on indulging, not wanting to make any effort, and deceiving to get what they want. Cheating, to them, represents a superiority. "Putting one over others" is particularly valued.

As they go along, as they move further and further away from any realness, their hollowness and crappiness becomes more and more apparent to them. Refusing to acknowledge their thoroughly stupid choices, they instead double-down, adding ever-increasing deceit to their distortions. Until everything they do is a lie, as they chase the impossibility of trying to bullshit their way out of the prison-of-non-being they've created for themselves.

"Age-old patterns are finally being discerned and exposed."

Bullshit has been around forever, since the first time someone tried to gain an unethical advantage. Today however, in the information age, we're in a position we've never been in before. We now have access to pattern and history. Everything is recorded in some way. We leave trails online, even if not done so ourselves. Others talk about us, take pictures or videos of us, or in other ways document what we do.

Besides this record, our access to information, especially truths, has exponentially multiplied. Yes, we might grumble at the overload of online bullshit, but when we encounter real truth through awareness, insight, discernment, and understanding, we're changed. The internet has accelerated the spreading of these understandings significantly.

We enter discussions or observe them much more frequently than we did before the internet. All of this results in a greater societal awareness. It's also led to greater mis-beliefs by those susceptible to bullshit, but even they eventually run into someone, or some discussion, where their foolish positions and beliefs are shown to be exactly that, bullshit. For many this is a shock and a rude awakening, sometimes traumatic. In the overall, society is waking up. More and more as a society we're seeing and recognising bullshit for what it is, a cancer on us, and society, slowly and perpetually eating away. The horror of this, especially when we're faced with undeniable truths, accumulates until it erupts into action.

The explosion of awareness about sexual harassment and abuse, and the resulting actions which are being taken, is a great example. Sexual harassment is extreme and harmful bullshit, further enabled by the complicit bullshit of others. Perhaps we ourselves have been one of those who enabled, through our silence or non-action.

In the online world, we can find others, find allies, find those who will stand with us. We don't have to deal with matters alone anymore. We can share our discernment and understanding, we can share our experiences, we can share our resistance and outrage, we can share our non-acceptance, and thereby we can make a difference. Times are changing, and they're changing fast.

"Complicity isn't an option! Character, integrity, and ethics are crucial! Appropriate-intolerance is now the order of the day! We need to step up!"

When dealing with severe bullshit which results in physical or financial harm, we can point to their visible consequence and force solutions. With more generalised and subtle bullshit, where the harm isn't so obvious, dealing with those negative results directly is more difficult.

In this age, we've greater access to the powerful weapons

of awareness and discernment since now we can all *share* our understandings. These discernments and understandings enter the general consciousness when sufficiently shared. This is how bullshit is going down! It can't exist where there's awareness of what it is, of how it works. The egregious example of an extreme bullshit-manipulator-narcissist on the world stage only serves to hasten the social revolution which is happening.

We like to ask, "But what can I do?" The answer is simply to act with character, integrity, and ethics. If we apply these incredibly powerful tools-of-being, we can only realise when it comes to bullshit, we actually have to be *intolerant*. A new understanding to sweep the world is: *appropriate-intolerance!*

As good people, we tend to automatically be tolerant, believing it to always be a good quality, but it's not always good. To be tolerant of evil is obviously not good. The problem with bullshit is it's not obviously bad until we fully understand, then we see just how bad it really is. Once we see bullshit for the cancer and blight it is, we realise intolerance is called for. Our intolerance when it comes to this disease is entirely appropriate.

It's difficult within the context of this book to make all the connections we'd like. To fully understand, unfortunately, we have to delve in-depth into the details of cock-eyed psychology. Otherwise the focus too quickly shifts to the positive replacements. Yes, those replacements are vital, and necessary, imperative. But they're not the focus of this work directly.

First those negatives have to be fully understood, to be undone and dealt with, to be unhooked from. Otherwise, we simply overlay a surface on a fragile base. Without that solid understanding of primitive or limited thinking, legacy beliefs and logic, we're vulnerable via our unawareness of what all is involved.

Opposite-Logic

"To discern root intent, we have to understand the complexity behind simplicity."

Bullshitters hide behind the simplicity of their facade, usually a facade which portrays them as being valuable in some way, even if it's only the small value of being "friendly." The bullshitter will go to great pains to hide themselves in a shroud of artlessness. Always they push this idea, because they're anything but simple. As is so often true of bullshitters, what they pitch is the exact opposite of what's accurate, and usually that opposite applies to *them*. If we pay attention to what bullshitters say and do, we can see how they completely give themselves away through this habit of pushing the opposite to conceal their bullshit.

If they call another a liar, it's because they're the liar. If they make a fuss about how dishonest someone is, it's because they're the dishonest one. If they point out how pathetic someone else is, what a "loser" they are, it's because they're the pathetic loser. It's the reality of the bullshitter; they give themselves away because their only option to avoid exposure is bullshit.

The more they attempt to divert our attention from the awful truth of what they are, the more they reveal themselves. Understanding this opposite logic of bullshit is a powerful tool-of-discernment for seeing into bullshitters.

"It is a profound act to see what is. To look at things for what they are. To be aware and make conscious the unseen, the obscure, the covert, the deliberately hidden. To observe beliefs, convictions, habituations, motivations,

and patterns. Therein lies the crux. Seeing winter coming is critical for dealing with it."

CH15 - Disturbing Implications

"Here he is Sir. He's been deep under-cover for a long time. Hanging with the bullshitters. Immersed in bullshit. I'm not sure we can get him back!"

Timid Criminality

"This was interesting, in that all forty psychopathic traits can pertain to someone - quite startling. However, there's one very very important factor: their behaviour can be ameliorated by timidity, which makes a huge difference! A saving grace for some bullshitters, to some extent. But timidity can be emboldened via associates and association."

Psychopaths are, of course, also bullshitters, but bullshitters aren't necessarily psychopaths. There's a difference, even though there's significant overlap. All the traits of the psychopath can apply to a bullshitter, but they still aren't a psychopath. The main reason: timidity. The bullshitter doesn't cross that line into the outright criminality we associate with the common conception of a psychopath. (The clinical definition doesn't necessarily mean criminality.)

Usually the bullshitter is too fearful of consequence. One of their prime motivations for bullshit is to avoid consequence. Their bullshit is exactly geared to avoiding preciseness and definitive judgements. It's risk aversion.

Bullshitters go to great pains to avoid saying or doing anything which can be definitively "proved." They thrive on the confusion of obfuscation. Implication is their chief weapon, as they then can't directly be held responsible. Always they can revert to saying, "But that's not what I said! You're just *interpreting* it that way." Or similar such machinations. In this way they escape direct condemnation. Their habit of avoiding determining acts and statements keeps them away from criminal acts in general.

This doesn't mean they're averse to criminality; they aren't. It's only their timidity in this regard which holds them at bay. When we fully understand the bullshitter, and the bullshit-manipulator-narcissist especially, there are disturbing implications.

Plotting and Scheming

"The way bullshit-manipulators 'relate' and interact reveals a plotting and scheming intent, a pre-determined agenda. There's nothing 'casual,' 'spontaneous,' or 'friendly' about these preconceived manipulations."

Let's assume a typical interaction, one which may lead to some sort of relationship beyond casual acquaintance. We come into contact with someone new. We know nothing about them. They're friendly and behave normally. We're given no indication this isn't so.

They take an interest in us, and this we like, we're
flattered. Our interest in them is now heightened. All
seems well and fine.

After a few interactions we notice small oddities,
peculiarities, nothing at all serious. Trivial, minor. We put
these down to the usual, that not everything is going to be
perfect. It's to be expected. Besides, they really like us,
they pay attention to us, are nice to us. We take things for
what they *seem* to be.

Implications, unfortunately here, are since in the context
of the book, this person is likely going to turn out to be a
bullshit-manipulator-narcissist. The implication is we need
to expect and potentially look at everyone as a potential
BMN. This absolutely does*n't* have to be so. We don't
have to go around suspecting everyone we meet. All we
need to be aware of, is the *possibility.* That's enough
usually.

If we add an understanding and a full detailed look at just
one BMN, after that we'll recognise the clues easily. Once
we know, it's obvious. The obvious is always so after we
become aware. Here lies the value of this book, to make
recognising a bullshitter obvious.

"Corrupt goals and motivations birth corrupt methods."

In our newly formed relationship, since we now
know about bullshitters, since we can now recognise them
and understand their underlying logic, we start to see
things differently. Their motivations and intents show. We
see when they're being nice to us, their objective isn't
really to make us happy, but it's all about how it makes
them look. We see how they jockey for status, even status
relative to us. We see their assumptions, how they take for
granted they're "superior" and other such nonsense. We
see how they have an agenda. Once we notice those
agendas, their bullshit is easy to recognise.

Most important, we ask, "What's their intent here?" Just asking this question makes all the difference. Just asking reveals that intent. Or enough to make it clear their intent is all about them, all about pretence, all about bullshit.

We're focused here on implication. Once we see this new "friend" is all about self-promotion, using, pretending, manipulating, and how they are only intent on the rubbish of the bullshitter, we see any real relationship is an impossibility. Always, if we look a bit further with such individuals, we end up at the implications of crappy intent.

Deliberate Schemes

"When the goal is indulgence, it reveals a corrupt mindset."

Once we've recognised a bullshitter, usually the most expedient course of action is to terminate all interactions and any relationship. In the interests of our learning and awareness, it's most useful to hang on for just a bit to observe the behaviour. Especially to observe the implications. Until we actually see for ourselves, implications are just theoretical. Once we see them play out, once we see that reality come about, then we *know, and* we provide ourselves an opportunity to develop trust in our perceptions and understandings.

Watching a bullshitter in action once we know what they're up to reveals disturbing implications. We get to see how everything they do is a deliberate scheme. We see how they always have their agenda of self first, their agenda of creating an image, of getting something for nothing, their agenda of dominance, and all the other pathetic intents they have.

"Bullshitters are perpetual and chronic opportunists jumping at every glimmer of chance out of necessity, as their lack of skill and abilities, their reliance on bullshit, and thus their insecurity forces this incessant greed for unearned reward."

The disturbing part is to see how deliberate it all is, how ever-present these motivations, agendas and intents are. How they *know* they're bullshitting. How they *know* they're false and phoney. How crappy and squirrelly and unethical they are. Yet they do what they do anyway. Yet they deliberately bullshit and manipulate anyway. This is the disturbing part. That conscious deliberation. It's hard to believe or comprehend without seeing it for oneself.

Fortunately, we don't have to get into a relationship or interaction with a bullshitter to observe this. There are plenty opportunities on TV or online to observe this. Just being aware that when it comes to bullshit, there are disturbing implications is enough to enable our bullshit radar.

Shared Responsibility

"Trying to emotionally and energetically bully and coerce others into respecting you is astonishingly preposterous! And those who allow and buy into it are themselves ludicrous - they maintain the old system! They support and maintain a world-view that's unethical!"

Disturbing implications don't only apply to the bullshitter and the BMN; they could apply to us as well. For instance, if we buy into hierarchy and use the mechanisms of superiority, even if only a little bit, and think it's okay when we do it, but not okay when others do it to us, the implications for us aren't pretty. It works both ways. Even if we do "only a little," the disturbing implications are we help maintain a bullshit system, we're complicit and culpable in that corruption. When the BMN bullies and abuses someone else in that system, we are, by implication, also partly responsible.

Bullshit Posse

"When a bullshitter no longer feels the need to bullshit, when they feel they can get away with their indulgences without needing the cover of pretence, that's when they step fully into the realm of abuse."

Bullshitter-manipulator-narcissists especially are emboldened by support. The more their bullshit is pandered to, the more their ego and vanity is supported by sycophants and toadies, the more they come to believe their own delusion and the more emboldened they get. Those feeding this beast refuse to face the unhealthy implications involved until it's too late, and they become acutely aware of those devastating implications as the beast devours them. Most unhealthy.

Whenever encountering a bullshitter or a BMN with their own support group, be ultra wary. That restriction of timidity typically in play is no longer a protection. These bullshitters can be, or can become, capable of anything. It's here they start to cross over into outright criminality and become even more dangerous.

The implications of this stage are they no longer really need the bullshit. They have what they crave, they're dominant, they're being flattered, they're receiving all the attention, and once they realise they can bully and dominate with abandon, they let go of the need for the bullshit and allow their ugly selves to flourish. It's at this stage where gaslighting to control and "own" becomes an option. Disturbing implications indeed.

Impossible Relationships

"The comparative-mindset and the lack of self-honesty limits truly relating."

If we're perhaps tempted to enter a relationship with a bullshitter, we but need remember one disturbing implication: bullshitters are incapable of having a genuine relationship. It's just not possible. When the entirety of someone's purpose is to "sell" a false self, how can they be in a real relationship? The relationship will be with a phantom; how is it feasible? Not only is this a disturbing implication, but the bullshitter is focused *only* on themselves and getting out of the relations just what benefits them. They want it all. How can that work? It can't. Not for us anyway. Implications are powerful, if we don't shy away from those which are disturbing.

"'Blackholes' are a one-way deal unto themselves. There's no way to actually 'save' a blackhole. Love is light, and the more that's added, the more is absorbed, it's an impossibility. Any giving to a blackhole only adds to it. The only course of action is to avoid it entirely, to be out of its influence completely, and just let it do what blackholes do. They implode eventually, if not fed. That's their way, and that's what they choose. That grabbing and grabbing, that relentless taking, that's the joy of the blackhole."

It's worth repeating: implications are powerful tools, if we don't steer away from those which are disturbing.

An intent of this book is to change social consciousness by making it clear how serious and devastating bullshit is. Not a simple problem. For instance, certain perspectives on victims, such as, "the victim is also to blame" or "the victim must bear some responsibility." There are many who believe some version of this.

If someone is captured by slavers, it's out of their hands. A psychology can be similarly captured. Something the general public don't understand. BMNs are slavers like that. They deliberately go about enslaving another's psychology and being. Typically their victims have little choice. There are many disturbing implications when it comes to how bullshit plays out.

Most good people make the effort to look to more, to look past the crapola to more, to sensibility or spirituality. They're aware of the crappy side of humans, and the depths of it. In general, with most people, they're not aware of the full depths of certain psychologies. Unfortunately, this causes problems and has implications.

We just have to look at society's overall perspective and attitude to all the aspects of bullshit to see the superficial perspective of bullshit. Bullshit is "BS" to most. It's this poo-pooing of bullshit as a minor issue which enables the bullshitters, and which leads to BMNs, to their extremes, their abuse, and them getting away with it. All because of inadvertent complicity and unintended condoning, all through lack of full awareness of the severity of the issue. It really is a big deal.

"The preposterous, the unreal, the fake, the phoney, the frauds, - exist, yet are unreal."

Another instance of the deeper problem is the general assumed misogyny simply taken for granted by most men. For instance, they subscribe to hierarchy in some way to hugely varying degrees, but typically it's there.

Thing is, for most of them, women aren't included in that

hierarchy. They're not even conscious of this taken for granted misogyny. It's incredible bullshit. One huge reason why the focus of this book has to be tight. It's to make us, as a society, aware of the implications and consequences of those small bullshits, like that assumed inadvertent misogyny and how it ends up having severe and monumental consequences.

A big problem is the complexity of bullshit. It's not neat and tidy and linear. It's a massive sphere of complexity with many sides to it all. When that whole sphere is known and understood, dealing with bullshit is much simplified. But difficult to communicate.

The problem of bullshit is a particular one. To get out from it, we first have to immerse into it to understand its full complexity. Once we understand, the path for dealing with it and reducing it in society as a whole is obvious. When we understand the severe consequences of what seems benign and trivial, the overwhelming majority of us can't partake in those small seemingly insignificant actions of transgression or complicity when we know what they lead to. Most people *do* have conscience and ethics, but through lack-of-awareness these are unfortunately not always activated.

"When we fully understand the severity of a situation, we can no longer overlook or ignore."

Ch16 - Ethical Complications

Repeated Transgressing

"These bullshit-manipulators are people in our day-to-day lives, in our community, and out there in our world. They're there for themselves and their self-promotion. They 'play' everybody. Their con is always on. Some like to think themselves exempt, being quite fine with the fact that as long as they're not being preyed on, it's alright. How does that make it okay?"

The no-fault logic, or forgiveness philosophy, is one many love, aspire to, and see great value in. However, it only works if all participants have integrity. For the short-cut mentality, which is primary to the BMN, this is a fantastic opportunity to exploit, manipulate, abuse, and take from those who subscribe to this ideal or similar. They rub their hands with glee at the prospect of transgressing, then simply saying "sorry" and, once forgiven, and all is reset, to then repeat the transgression. They will do this over and over again, as long as they're allowed to get away with this thoroughly unscrupulous, unethical, and shitty behaviour.

Good people find it difficult to believe or comprehend someone could be so low and dastardly, and well, evil, when it comes to such behaviour, but if we're to be honest and apply our integrity to all of life, we have to acknowledge this sad reality exists.

Animal Psychology

"The onus is on us to deal with the inconvenient pressure of the emotional and energetic manipulations of the squirrelly, smarmy, conscienceless creatures in our midst, be they 'lover', 'friend', father, brother, sister, mother, colleague or neighbour."

We have to be careful in assuming all who look like humans are, in fact, typically or mostly human. Sometimes, even though they can be human their *behaviour* comes from an animal-like psychology.

An example of this mindset: a nice lady notices raccoons scavenging for food in her trash can. She feels sorry for them and leaves some food out. At first the raccoons are wary, nervous of the human. Soon they realise the nice lady will not, indeed cannot, hurt nor harm them. The nice lady is taken in by their "friendliness," allowing them into her home. The raccoons take advantage, and the nice lady forgives them, unable to assign responsibility or take negative seeming measures. She doesn't want to engage in "negativity' or unpleasantness. Pretty soon the raccoons realise this and end up taking over her home, pushing the nice lady out. Turning aggressive toward her as she tries to get at her own food for herself.

Sadly, many a well-meaning charity worker has had their heart, ideals, and psychologies crushed by just such circumstances, except, of course, with people. Niceness to some is the same as weakness, and is only to be exploited and taken advantage of.

Realistic Options

"There's no equality in chicken-land."

Admirable ideals are admirable, but only if they're tempered with sensibility and practical applicability, and especially, appropriateness. Applying an interactive philosophy and psychology meant for ethical humans with integrity, to the unethical or those with primitive mindsets is foolish and inappropriate. We need to keep this in mind when it comes to dealing with some people. Yes, they do have the *potential* for change, and positivity, but until such potential is realised, we have to act and behave according to what is, not according to what we wish for or hope for.

With that being said, if we have the energy, time, and circumstance, we *can* be instrumental in providing opportunity for others to act and behave in ways completely a-typical to them. We can even lead them, and in a positive way even guide their willingness to choose from more positive options of behaviour. A guidance toward an awareness of more choices. This is a behaviour which requires some skill and awareness of not-so-positive psychology, not to mention a degree of independence-of-being and awareness. But is certainly possible and doable.

"It is incumbent on us to not condone the squirrelly among us. - If we've inadvertently done so by being naive, trusting, and believing their lies, the lesson is to reserve

one's support until we're sure, and thereby not enabling the morally defunct among us through premature actions."

Unfortunately, the demands and pressures of our reality, the urgencies of circumstance, necessitate we use whatever tool is at our disposal. Usually, the most effective is simple avoidance. But to avoid we have to first recognise, and it's to this end much of this book is geared.

"If we can see trouble before it sees us, getting out of the way is easy."

Ch17 - Chaos-Profiteers

Contamination and Confusion

"Bullshit-manipulators don't just contaminate an environment; they destroy them. They're parasites who bring down the host, whoever and whatever that might be. Sowing chaos and 'excitement' to disrupt and seize opportunity for themselves."

Every minute, every second, of the BMN's life is filled with the pressure of pretence. They're under threat of exposure with every single utterance and behaviour. A constant stress which manifests in various ways, usually re-diverted negativity on those luckless enough to be deemed unworthy of the need to impress, charm, flatter, or whose attention doesn't matter.

This stress never relents, there's never any respite. They love chaos, for this is the one time nothing matters. In chaos they can do whatever, be whatever, and it doesn't matter. In chaos they can be unfettered and unrestrained, allowing their every indulgence to run wild. Chaos thus represents a release from that ever-present threat of exposure.

"Bullshit-manipulators love confusion because they can take charge and get away with their unsavoury objectives. There's a manic sense about getting a leg-up during chaos. The desire for chaos allows the unscrupulous to feel like they're 'leaders' who can 'do what they want,' dominating others and imposing otherwise untenable activities and intents. Chaos 'legitimises' bullshit. Who can tell bullshit from truth during chaos? It thus becomes simple and easier to appear relatively 'better.'"

Chaos represents massive opportunity to the BMN. They crave being "leaders" and "teachers," even gurus and such like, but they seldom possess the requisite abilities or want to make the appropriate efforts to justify being such people. Also, being in such positions magnifies potential scrutiny, and thus possible exposure. A conundrum and catch-22 for the BMN. In times of chaos, none of that matters. They know when everything is falling apart, *anyone* can be a "leader."

The BMN sees chaos as a fantastic opening, as in environments of disruption. It's whoever *seizes* the lead who gets the lead. Qualifications, history, reputation, character aren't an issue, as there generally isn't time or situation to check and verify. First in gets the plum. Mostly in circumstances of mayhem, people are just too happy *someone*, anyone, is taking charge and taking responsibility. Thus the BMN grabs this chance. They can jump in, bullshit flying, and be received with open arms.

Control

"Bullshitters like to cause emotional chaos, which they then take advantage of."

Chaos can represent family trauma, relationship break-ups, and other human drama scenarios, or the more usual kind of physical disaster. Chaos can also extend to economic and political circumstances, and here is where we can see dire examples of BMNs seizing power and control of very real assets, all because of bullshit. Once seized and dominance is cemented, they're extremely difficult to get rid of or dislodge. A serious matter. (We but need to look at how the oligarchs came to power to see the dangers of this opportunism.)

On a more local level, when the BMN does involve themselves, with discord or crisis, no matter how local or temporary, and we take note and observe what they *actually* accomplish, as opposed to what they propose or purport, inevitably we encounter a ridiculous incompetency. Seldom can the bullshitter live up to their own hype. Because nothing in their lives has ever been genuine. Real skills and abilities are likewise scarce. They become victims of their own bullshit through convincing themselves they're more than they really are. But when illusion meets reality, their hollowness is revealed.

It's deeply ironic how the BMN craves chaos to relieve the constant pressures and fear of exposure, but when this eventuality occurs, it usually leads to the very exposure they dread. Unfortunately, the cost for us of this discovery is typically high. During disarray, we need to be especially wary of those excited by turmoil, by those who all too readily volunteer to take charge or who simply push themselves into positions of leverage unasked. If we don't object and thwart these attempts at control and dominance, we've only ourselves to blame.

Shitpile Logic

"Being in the muck removes need for all the pretence of maintaining illusion, lies, and deception. Relieving the pressures of preserving the appearance of good. The actually negative scenario is now perceived as relatively positive by comparison. This is when bullshitters get caught by their own bullshit, ending up immersed and swallowed by their own foolishness."

A further appeal of chaos is the levelling of hierarchy, that all-important relative superiority which usually is only of critical importance to the bullshitter. In their minds, chaos reduces everyone to nothing, chaos brings everyone down to their level. This levelling delights them, they salivate at the prospect, for it relieves another pressure, the constant pressure they feel of being "inferior." Their continual feelings of lacking, their intense dislike and resentment of this believed lesserness is what drives them to cover their failings via bullshit. However, when normalcy is upended, they're now suddenly "equal."

They don't believe in equality. It's a state which doesn't exist for them, because anytime there's "equality," it provides an easy opportunity to position themselves relatively "higher," to thus dominate and be "superior" with little effort. A great appeal to the bullshitter. They can easily "look good" and be relatively "better." For the BMN, chaos represents an ideal opportunity to manipulate and control, and for once, be on top.

Chaos Vigilance

"When chaos is afoot, no matter how minor or local, we need take special care, be extra vigilant."

Bullshitters will actively seek to create and foment chaos. They're quite happy to cause widespread disadvantage to others, all for their potential personal benefit. It's a monstrous mentality, one almost impossible for good people to believe or even conceive. Once we realise this lunacy, once we become aware these psychologies exist, we recognise the many examples which abound of just exactly this incredible moronity, the very pinnacle of bullshit.

Historic examples, or those which make the news, are easy enough to spot, but we need to make the effort to notice when these happen in our immediate lives. All too often we refuse to believe what's going on right in our laps, because it's just too crazy. We can't afford to fall into the trap of only believing the absurdity once it's too late. We can't wait for conclusive "proof." We have to act when we see the signs and symptoms of deceit. Usually there's more than enough warning. Only if we pay attention and direct our awareness to the intricacies and implications of bullshit.

"Seeing things for what they are is a skill not everyone chooses to employ."

The totality of deception, for some caught up in it, is hard to believe. But when we actually see it, day in, day out, we get to know that's how it is. Even if it takes a while.

The problem for the bullshitter is it's they who created their distorted reality, a problem of their own doing. They've elevated appearance, image, and status to such ridiculous levels of importance they can only become obsessed with the maintenance of their bullshit facades, which suck them in and become their world.

It doesn't in the least have to be so. It's all because of their choice to believe foolish beliefs.

We absolutely don't like absolutes. In this, it's exactly our difficulty in believing, which is the problem when it comes to dealing with people like this. That reluctance to accept this awful truth is what leads to entanglement, giving chances, hope of change, and all sorts of other debilitating consequences.

Yes, there's always hope, hope which needs to be applied from a distance. There's always hope the lion won't eat you. But it's generally more prudent not to test that chance by being up close and personal.

When one is entangled with a BMN, that absoluteness matters absolutely, as it's vital to understand the totality of their disease. For that's what it is. A disease of ego, of narcissism, of insecurity and inferiority. A disease of mis-belief. Their immersion has made it a totality, the delusion of a bubble, which isn't a complete reality. It's their complete world to them. That's what matters.

"Refusing to acknowledge the absoluteness of addiction to bullshit is dangerous."

Gaslighting

"The utter refusal to acknowledge wrongdoing or mistake can lead to the rearrangement of their entire world."

Emboldened bullshitters and BMNs create chaos in various ways from which to benefit. One such is gaslighting, the subversion, distortion, and rearrangement of truth for another. Not only does it create an internal chaos and confusion for the other, or others, from which they benefit via easier manipulation, but also the thrill, for them, of complete and total control of another. This makes them feel he cleverest and most power being in the world. Ridiculous and sad, but unfortunately real.

"Gaslighting is the ultimate in bullshit."

Anther reason gaslighting comes to be used is more petty, it's when there's just no way out of their bullshit and lies and thus they will double down exponentially to the extreme. If they can obfuscate the truth, well, then it's hard to "prove" their perfidy and now the lies, bullshit, distortions, deceits and manipulations are no longer so glaringly obvious. Profit from chaos indeed.

"Goodness automatically comes with inherent humility, which leads to an acceptance we may be wrong. A loophole of doubt to be exploited by the conscienceless."

If we are ever in a situation where we come to question our reality and sanity becomes someone is leveraging our innate and appropriate openness to doubt, beware, this is the fulcrum point the gaslighter will manipulate to the extreme using all their tools and tricks as we have discussion, such as preposterousness, obfuscation etc. Gaslighting is when the restraints are off, or they are extremely desperate and they need to or come to use all their manipulations. An extremely dangerous situation where distance and perspective are your saviours, as this fog of chaos only survives if constantly fed and controlled.

"When in doubt, run."

Ch18 - Truth-Aversion

Avoidance

"Those who fool and delude themselves usually think they fool and delude everyone."

The mindset of the bullshitter is geared to avoiding truth. The awful truth, the uncomfortable truth, awkward truth, unpleasant truth, inconvenient truth. Any truth not suitable to them, they avoid. They suffer from truth aversion because they believe, and for the most part it's true, that the truth doesn't favour them, and it doesn't. Instead of dealing with the reality of themselves, like the rest of us, learning and growing as needed, they instead try to obliterate their personal truth with lies.

"You're as tolerant as you are tolerable." - The Young Man

Bullshitters have to do a lot of extra work. Bullshit is like that; it's a bad joke on the bullshitters. Their idea is to avoid the efforts of learning, and instead they end up spending much more effort on pushing and maintaining their charade and avoiding the threat of exposure. Intolerance of themselves makes them negative toward people in general. They believe their real selves are at the bottom, and believe bullshit will help them change that status.

These mis-beliefs, along with many others, envelop them in a bubble-of-misery, where they have to constantly either pull down or suppress others to make themselves look relatively better. As a consequence, they create a truth which is vastly worse than the reality. They end up in a shitpile of their own creation where they aren't tolerated or liked because they aren't tolerable and likeable, leading to ever-increasing bullshit efforts to "fix" this problem. It's a no-win for them.

"Meanness can be a short-cut."

Bullshit is not benign. There's some truth-aversion by us when it comes to this. Bullshit is deception, there's no way around this uncomfortable truth. The deception is one of trying to convince us they're nice, cool, friendly, helpful, and all manner of other untrue pretence. Why? Why do they feel the need to deceive us?

Because they believe what they are isn't enough, is lacking, is deficient. Their belief, based largely on their incessant comparison, causes them to constantly feel "less than," inferior, lacking. A perpetual pressure on their ego leading to resentments, jealousies, and an ongoing meanness and nastiness, which they take great pains to hide, except when they feel it's "safe" to let it out. Typically in private situations where they feel dominant and have some measure of control and power.

These are truths of the bullshitter and the BMN. Bullshitters have an aversion to these truths. It's their failing and fatal flaw. If we don't want to be infected by the cancer of bullshit, these hard truths are truths we absolutely cannot avoid or ignore.

Ignorant Envy

"Jealousy is proof of internal self-perceptions and beliefs which aren't favourable."

We but need observe bullshitters to see the jealousy seep from them. They can't help it. They live in a continual state of wanting what others have, what others are. Seldom can they obtain these wants. Bullshit simply isn't capable of delivering. Yes, they might acquire the outward trappings of success, but internally, they can't hide from the truth of their hollowness.

Even worse, the more successful they become, the worse the truth is for them. What happens when one has wealth and status, and it still doesn't make you happy? What happens when you're successful and wealthy and you don't have real friends, if you aren't really liked or enjoyed? What happens if all your success is based on a lie? How can you possibly feel good about it? You can't.

Bullshitters are completely self-defeating. If they succeed, it only brings them misery. What an awful truth to live with, knowing nothing you do will bring you happiness.

Sexual Immaturity

"To those attuned to the language of the bedroom, rarely does it lie."

Peculiar realities about the bullshitter are revealed in the bedroom. Here their truth aversion catches up with them, as it's exceedingly difficult to maintain bullshit when intimacy is the focus. Not that they won't try, but it's too apparent and obvious to sustain. If there's repeated intimacy, they will tend to revert to their bullshitless state-of-being, which is a child. A truth which makes for awkward and immature sexual interactions.

"Bullshitters reveal themselves by what they 'push.' Two elements in particular are their 'sexual prowess' and that they have friends. Always the implications they imply with this pretence is that they 'have' something."

Bullshitters are closely attuned to what they believe others think is cool and to what they imagine will get them approval and attention. Two such beliefs are having sexual prowess and having friends. They push this particular pretence in a way which reveals their overall self-hype strategy. The strategy of implication. When pushing they have sexual prowess, by implication, they push that they *have* sex, lots of it. Further, by implication, if they're having lots of sex, they "must be" sexually attractive, or just attractive in general.

Why not push this directly? Because they can easily be called on pushing attractiveness directly. Unless they have movie star appeal, which they seldom do, this is an obvious bullshit, the truth of it plain. If this is pushed *by implication* via sexual prowess, the truth of it is hard to determine. An indirect technique they use in all areas of their personal propaganda.

"When everything is all about the self, sexual prowess is an impossibility."

The myth of sexual prowess is one they need to push, because the underlying truth is sexual ability, or even any kind of real intimacy, is an improbability for them as their entire focus is solely on themselves. That's all they care about, all they're interested in promoting or hiding. How can they possibly make another happy if they're only thinking about themselves?

Even when they try, their actions are a lie, and their falseness always has the same goal, promote the bullshitter in some way. Their actions are never genuinely geared to another's happiness, and in the case of sex, it matters not how many sexual "tricks' they've learned. These are all hollow and false, and thus don't have the desired effect. They can't. Intimacy, and real sexuality, requires genuineness.

"'Performing' isn't compatible with lovemaking."

Everything for the bullshitter is a perpetual performance. Not only are they constantly performing, but they're performing as a false person. When the self isn't real, how can there be an intimacy? What would we be intimate with when this is attempted with a bullshitter? Intimacy is simply not possible with a false persona. Intimacy is only possible with real people. This is its appeal. A truth the bullshitter fails to understand. Or avoids facing at all costs.

"The very fact sexual prowess is being pushed indicates the contrary."

If we look and listen to the reports of women who have been sexually abused and harassed, particularly by famous and "successful" individuals, a few oddities stand out when it comes to these interactions with bullshitters, or more typically, bullshit-manipulator-narcissists. Usually there's a gross ineptitude when it comes to sexual advances or seduction. A peculiarity, especially when coming from physically attractive individuals.

For instance, when the attempted seduction is via some form of genital exposure, affected "accidentally." The entire business often has as its basis a childish element, a lack of confidence, and a decided lack of any sexual prowess. The very fact they have to, and try to, leverage their status and power to get sex reveals their absolute ineptitude in this regard, as well as their general insecurity. Why?

When one is utterly fake and phoney, when there's no reality of being, when everything is a cover-up of the internal hollowness, how can there be any real ability to connect with others in a real and intimate way? They only know 'tricks' to get approval and attention. They never, all their lives, learned how to truly connect. Thus, when it comes to sexual interaction, they fail miserably and resort to leveraging their status and power via some manipulation or trick.

Even then, they can't even really do this effectively. They simply don't have anything real with which to have normal sexual interactions. Never mind intimacy. If we look closely at the sexual abusers and harassers, we see deeply insecure, lonely, miserable people, besides severely lacking honesty, conscience, and ethics. A truth-aversion they fail to avert, an impossibility when it comes to truth.

"Bullshit isn't only a cancer on society, it's a severe cancer of the self, of the soul, and, like cancer, eventually kills its host."

Ch19 - Consequences

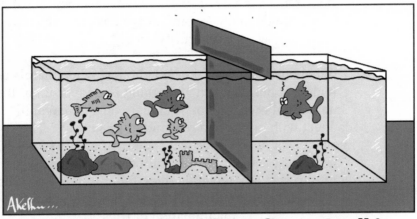

"I had it custom made to fit.. .. I call it a 'Bullshitter avoidance screen' !!"

Contamination

"Bullshit-manipulators are like sheep who shit in their drinking water. Before long, that water is totally fouled, becoming undrinkable."

Bullshitters are so immersed in their phoney worlds, they lose connection with the real world. Their incessant fabrication disconnects them, resulting in a severe contraction of perception. Like sheep, a constant problem is fouling their environment through lack of awareness. If constantly pushing out figment, which is crap and rubbish, how can their world not become contaminated? Unfortunately, those self-absorbed sheep, so focused only on their own immediate self-gratification, also foul and poison the water for everyone.

"The bullshit mindset is a square-circle psychology, an inherently contradictory belief system."

Seeing, knowing, recognising, and being aware of bullshit and bullshitters is important, otherwise we inadvertently end up in their foul worlds. Bullshitters need to get out of the pond, or we have to. Leaving them to eliminate themselves with their own corruption. We can't allow ourselves to be contaminated. They're so convinced fabrication and its supposed benefits are the way to go, they become lost in their bubbles of mis-belief, making them unable to see the very real negative consequences. Negative consequences especially to themselves. In fact, the bullshitter is usually the greatest loser. They never realise living in a world comprised entirely of bullshit is living in a dung heap.

Blindspots

"Bullshit-manipulators cause much harm. They're flat-out unethical. Their bullshit is serious contamination, tipping the balance toward the detrimental and the chaotic to benefit and prosper. They will self-promote from the very disruptive, seemingly exciting air they institute. Bullshitters are polluters, corrupters, and destabilisers without conscience!"

Bullshitters lie and distort with abandon, but they're not too concerned with being perceived as doing so. Not in the way normal people are. It's a peculiarity, somewhat of an anomaly. It's so obvious mostly they're lying and bullshitting, yet they seem unconcerned by this. Their unconcern stems from the knowledge that should they be called out specifically, they can squirm their way out of trouble. Most of what they say is non-specific enough to allow them to claim they were misunderstood, or they misspoke, or some other fudging.

When they're confronted with an undeniable factual untruth, they simply blame it on someone else. They "heard" it somewhere or they were "told" by someone. Always it will be someone else's fault, never theirs. They know they can shift blame and responsibility easily, and thus aren't too worried about this aspect of their pretence.

"Bullshit is a fiction to maintain the illusion of not having transgressed against conscience."

The negative effects on their reputation and the perceptions of others of them in this regard isn't part of their usual narcissistic concern. A blindspot, but necessary. They have to con themselves it doesn't matter. As long as no one can "prove" conclusively they're lying, it doesn't overly concern them. To further ameliorate the negative effects of their deceit and distortion, they just carry on as if it's no problem at all, even when it's obvious they've lied or have been bullshitting.

This vibe they foster, that their dishonest confabulations are nothing and never were anything goes a long way to dampening and even cancelling any negative effect, as most people tend to have fairly short memories and trend with the current mood and vibe. Also, the bullshitter knows most people don't like to hold negativity too long, and in the face of good cheer and their "friendliness," it's difficult for most to hang onto past, somewhat unpleasant, behaviours, which weren't particularly clear.

"Bullshitters, as people, ultimately just make no sense at all. They cannot."

Of course, if we pay but just a bit of attention, we spot the pattern, and that pattern is more than enough to condemn the bullshitter. Regardless of specific proof, after a while the probabilities they're bullshitting and lying simply become too high to ignore. That is, if we have the ethical fortitude to act on what we know. *WE* have to enact consequence by cutting out the bullshitters from our lives, and refusing to interact and thus be forced to deal with their crap and nonsense. WE need to be selective and responsible. The bullshitter most certainly will not.

Expectations

"The distorted world of bullshit and its attempt at 'specialness' distorts reality, making true togetherness a practical impossibility!"

The bullshitter tries to push a persona and being they believe is advantageous. It's also untrue, false, phoney, and unreal. How they imagine this can actually result in real relationships is a mystery. It's not so mysterious when we realise they simply don't think matters through. In this regard they don't think ahead, or if they do, they just figure they will fabricate their way out of any difficulties.

How can one be intimate? How can one truly share and connect with another? How can one experience the benefits of a close and intimate relationship if there's no realness of being? It can't happen. An impossibility. What a sad consequence of bullshit.

"When our perception changes, we change. When the obfuscations, omissions, and hyperbole are revealed, we see clearly. We can make better decisions, live better lives."

The positive consequences for us from learning to recognise and understand disguised deception lies in freedom from entanglements. We aren't sucked in. Not only that, but seeing it coming allows us to get out of the way and avoid involvement with corruption altogether.

"Sometimes giving 'a dog a good name' causes them to run amuck."

A somewhat unexpected consequence involving bullshitters BMNs comes from inappropriate positivity. Many of us prefer, as a matter of goodness, to have a positive expectation of others when we know nothing about them. For the BMN, this results in them having a kind of free reign. They abuse that positive expectation in them, exploiting and manipulating this false belief for all it's worth.

They understand good people will stick with that positive "good name" and assumption as long as possible, thus giving them time to employ their bullshit. For instance, using this attributed positivity to "get in" with friends and business associates, that sort of bullshit. All trading on your goodness, good reputation, and good name. In the end the consequence for you is to be tainted by association.

"The preposterousness of bullshit has no limit."

When the bullshitter or BMN is discovered and seen for what they are, clear and active disassociation is needed. Friends and business associates have to be made aware the actions of the bullshitter are in no way endorsed nor supported by us, and we're completely not in agreement with them. The harm is typically already done, damage control our only option. It's sad we can't always assume the best in others, and we don't want this to be our habit either. We don't want to live life always being suspicious of everyone.

Once we learn the ins and outs of bullshit and how it works, it's relatively easy to spot bullshitters, even before they say or do much. Typically, if we simply ask, "What's the agenda and intent here?" The answers are obvious and clear. We might not be able to say for sure what's said is bullshit, but when combined with the intent and agenda, it becomes clear. Just knowing we're dealing with bullshit is enough to prevent the negative consequences. Usually those only happen if we involve ourselves with bullshitters.

"The biggest problem is their subversive nature and the underground pervasive negativity of their being, which is their personal climate. And then there's one's own natural inclination to want to turn a negative into positive. Which doesn't truly work with them, just creating complicity, entanglement, and a strange kind of acquiescence to their hierarchical bullshit."

A consequence of automatic friendliness to bullshitters is becoming enmeshed. Once involved, it's complicated to unentangle. The bullshit is all so nebulous, vague, and involved. Nothing is clear. It's difficult knowing what to uninvolve from. Our best course of action is to cut all ties completely. Avoid *ANY* interaction whatsoever, no matter how trivial.

This might seem harsh and over-reactive. But the bullshitter will seek to exploit any small chance or gap we leave. The worst downside is our complicity in "supporting" their bullshit. Even if only by association. We support them just by maintaining a connection and friendliness, however small.

"There's no real value to prevarication. The supposed value of deceptive fiction is based purely on short-term, temporary apparent benefits, and is a myth. Bullshitters in the end actually suffer the most from their own bullshit."

The key to understanding bullshitters is seeing past the surface. Looking more than one step ahead. Not becoming sucked into the immediate and *apparent* idea, mood, vibe, and energy pushed by the bullshitter. Paying attention to the actual costs and consequences of the bullshit persona reveals a different picture. We see their inability to have relationships, their misery and unhappiness. How can they be happy with a fake self? It's not real, and never will be. How can this result in any happiness? They face constant stress and pressure from needing to maintain their bullshit, and from their constant fear of exposure. All consequences severely negative in the long term.

"Bullshitters crave success, elevation, status, importance, but at the same time fear these, as the risks of exposure are magnified. They live in a hell of no-win consequence. The result of adopting bullshit as a solution to their problems and desires."

The worst of it is that if they actually get what they aim for, their success becomes their undoing. For instance, most bullshit is geared toward self-promotion, making the bullshitter out to be more than they are.

If for some reason they succeed and someone buys what they sell, and they end up in a situation or circumstance where they need to be what they've claimed, they cannot fulfil this promise, revealing they're not only a liar, but incompetent as well. Not to mention exposing their underlying lack of honesty and ethics. So they lose massively if they get what their fiction tries for. The overwhelming consequence of bullshit is a no-win scenario for the bullshitter.

"The prevalence of bullshit has resulted in a plague of incompetence."

The myth of value from phoney pretending is exactly that, a myth. This false belief of value keeps the bullshitter going, and all for nothing. A sad irony. A problem with short-sighted, short-cut, and immediate-benefit thinking. They fail to see the futility of waiting for the impossible benefit of trying to turn untruth into truth. There's no future to deception; this they refuse to acknowledge. Once caught up in pretence, they have to keep piling on more and more to sustain the myth. Bullshit is its own horrendous consequence, an expectation with no hope of success.

"When considering the harm bullshit causes, we're well served to understand why drip-water torture is one of the worst. It's continuous, unrelenting, ever-present, coming in little bits at a time, but individually, seem harmless."

Ch20 - Counteracting Awareness

Awareness Power

"There has to be discomfort with courage, because when we're being courageous, there IS some risk. Risk is threat. Risk should make us a bit uncomfortable. If not, we're fools. That discomfort is what keeps us alert, ready, alive. It's a necessary component of courage, and of trust. We can take solace from that, to know those odd feelings are the feelings which come from being courageous." - Biella Noble

Once we know, once we understand, once we're able to recognise and see, this knowing is reflected in our awareness. That kind of awareness is typically enough to put off the BMN from even trying their nonsense with us.

They know what they're doing, they know it's not kosher,

they know what they peddle and push can't hold up to scrutiny, especially the scrutiny of someone who's able to perceive and understands the finer points and techniques of bullshit.

"There are times in the lives of good people when it's appropriate to be disapproving, because to be anything other could be misconstrued as condoning and complicity."

The BMN actively looks for lack of awareness, that certain naivete and immersiveness into non-awareness. They're selective when and with whom they ply their rubbish. The old saying, "Victims invite aggression," can be adapted to "the unaware invite bullshit." Not to mention invite being taken advantage of.

It's of no use to simply be aware bullshit exists and is "out there." We need detailed inside knowledge of exactly how it works to enable us to see and recognise bullshit before it even gets a chance to act. There's a certain look in the eye and feel to the demeanour and presence of people who are "in the know." It's a real thing, a realness the bullshitter has to avoid. Bullshit cannot exist where realness is paramount.

That projection of knowing comes from their awareness, their being, from actually understanding what's what. One doesn't have to possess all the facts. Those are easy to research, especially in today's world. Knowing what's what when it comes to personal interactions comes from being able to tell when facts are being misused, or when statements are made which simply assume facts not in evidence, and so on. Likewise with distortings, spin, hype, implication, innuendo, etc. Once we know, it's easy to recognise. This is the power of understanding and awareness.

"The awareness that bullshit is neither innocuous nor

trivial is powerful."

Awareness is a powerful force, especially in interpersonal interactions. We overwhelmingly tend to suppress our awareness when dealing with others. Why? Because we don't want them to see what we're thinking! Especially if our thoughts aren't totally positive. Think about that for a second.

Applying this to oneself, we realise how much we can potentially give away with our awareness alone. Just the same, we can give away what we wish, to pre-emptively be of use to us.

"The way to circumvent subtle parasitic entanglement and entrapment of contrived complicity for the aim of false egoic approval and dominance-superiority is via appropriate disapproval of the individual beingness of the bullshit-manipulator."

The impact-of-awareness is an amazing force. It relies on honesty. Just try pushing an awareness of something you know nothing about. Doesn't work. For most people it's pretty much impossible. Thus, to make a difference with our awareness, like stopping BMN's before they even start, we actually have to have an understanding and insight into the ins and outs of BS.

Also, understanding how being aware, and how having awareness of something, impacts and affects our interactions helps us understand the mind of the BMN. They, too, have some understanding of how awareness works, and to this end, they always first have to bullshit themselves in some way. Or a part of themselves. This is how they get around the integrity of awareness, or try to. They always first convince themselves of their points or angles. This inner-deception sets the bullshitter apart.

"One has to look very carefully at underlying agenda and

intent, rather than surface blather. Typically there's a discrepancy between what's conveyed, and the actuality which is personal to each individual. This discrepancy is usually large when the divergent agendas are askew."

Of course they try and get away with their inner bullshit, but can't. There's always a part of them which knows. They keep trying because they insist on getting what they want despite the means used. They develop separate sides to themselves, the honest side gets deeply buried under all the bullshit. Even with that deep burial, its influence is always there, coming through as a falseness and insincerity, easy to spot if we're looking, if we're open, if we're aware.

"As long as bullshitters appear pleasant on the surface, they're inappropriately tolerated by good people. What's required is appropriate intolerance. In the home! In the community! Everywhere!"

It's thus we can counteract bullshit with awareness. Especially with the awareness of the preposterousness that's the foundation of bullshit. Once we're aware there *ARE* people who do these kinds of things and they're among the people of our everyday lives, it changes us, changes our awareness, and with it, changes our interactions, adding us to those who change the world for the better, simply through being aware.

Understanding and Truth

"There's dire need in our society to not tolerate unethical jackasses. There's dire need in our society to go beyond complicity and the condoning of the ethically compromised. There's dire need in our society to be cognisant of energetic polluters of wholesome situations and to have an unbiased awareness of the preposterous."

To fully identify, we need to understand. The two are intimately connected, otherwise it's shallow and doesn't lead to any possibility of remedy or resolution. One can't always resolve. We might not have the time, ability, opportunity etc. to actually influence a bullshitter's behaviour directly. Also, we have to be careful with excusing, as excusing is also being complicit in perpetrating.

Our focus with this book is geared to removing all inadvertent implied condoning, via comprehension. Through thorough understanding, there's no possibility of co-opted enabling. What bullshitters and especially bullshit-manipulator-narcissists do, cannot be accepted. But it can be understood. Understanding allows us to deal with the inexcusable without it being emotionally disruptive.

"What's incomprehensible for some isn't necessarily so for others. This particularly applies to the realm of ethics."

Think of a general leading a war. The enemy is bad, inexcusable. Do you want a general who's hateful and emotionally affected by the enemy? Or one who understands them to the extent they can approach dealing with them unemotionally and with clarity? The very presence of an awareness of what's going on is a remedy, or leads to solution. Bullshit can't operate and thrive where there's awareness of what it is, what it's doing, and how it works. It just falls flat under those conditions. Bullshit is a tricky enemy, but only if we're unaware.

Any time there's strong emotion, it distorts judgement. In a general, one doesn't want that. One wants understanding without disrupting emotion. Fully understanding the wrongness doesn't mean one has to be emotional about it. Actually, full understanding usually leads to the opposite.

Thorough understanding leads to action without the distractions of compromising emotion. Intense emotion leads to bubbles of immersion and the reduction of awareness, and thus severely limiting the ability to deal with the problem. Think again of the general. One wants her as aware as possible. Escalated emotion severely limits awareness, understanding expands awareness.

"Even the most preposterous of situations are incredible journeys into mystery."

How we feel all depends on our focus. There are two parts to ugly truth. If we only focus on the ugly, we only get ugly. Truth is always beautiful. Truth itself, no matter what it's about. If we focus on the beauty of truth, the beauty which brings us awareness and discernment, we can see the ugliness, if that's the truth, and know it, and learn without being touched by the ugliness, because we keep our focus on the beauty, on the awesomeness of truth. If we keep our focus on the magnificence of acquiring awareness, discernment, and understanding, all we see is the beauty part of ugly truth.

Ch21 - Remedy

**Surgical removal of the bullshit gland.
Extreme remedy number 33.**

"Got it!"

Emotional Sensibility

"You can't use logic on someone who's resigned to limiting their awareness."

When dealing with individuals who transgress in some way, especially those who transgress ethical boundaries or decency limits, and those who abuse their power, when dealing with those with whom saying something is problematic, there's something we need to be very aware of: our emotions! When dealing with these individuals, awareness unaffected by emotion is the most appropriate tool of choice.

"To deal with bullshit, be real."

When dealing with a BMN who's abusive, unpleasant, nasty, rude, aggressive, unreasonable, petty etc., reflecting and allowing our awareness of the situation to show is a marvellous tool. But! We can counteract every bit of value this has by adding into the mix our *emotional reactions.*

For instance, glumness, resentment, anger, etc. Yes, the emotions on our side are fully justified. We're dealing with a compromised psychology in the first place, so the usual rules of rationality, logic, reason, and sensibility already don't apply.

"Why do you need to feel bad if you're not guilty? That's bullshit logic."

Usually emotions, especially those like resentment, will only serve to *ADD* to the mistreatment as they will be taken as a critique. For these mindsets there's no possibility of admitting wrongdoing or of having ever been wrong in anything. Therefore, critique can't have the usual desired result of showing the mistake or wrong, and this awareness leading to correcting behaviour and change. Unlikely to happen with the psychologies we're dealing with here.

"Fighting bullshit with bullshit is a no-win scenario."

It's important to understand with this psychology, for them, being wrong is a gross no-no. Acknowledging and admitting is even worse. To the gross ego mentality, owning up is the most stupid thing one could possibly ever do. If others force you to look stupid, this they can still understand, as the other is, in their logic, gaining superiority in doing so. But to lower oneself in the hierarchy willingly, no! That's unthinkable.

We must understand their incredible sensitivity to perceptions of relative status. It's everything to them.

Their ego's reaction to fault is to deny, cover up, hide, obfuscate, etc. Also, typically when the wrong is clear and obvious, since acknowledgement is out of the question and options are limited, there's a kind of desperation which sets in, leading often, or even typically, to a *doubling-down* on the original behaviour.

"If there's an earnest intent, the path is revealed. The path is our daily circumstance, our daily interactions, the happenings and situations we find ourselves in. What we need is contained all around us, all the time. All we need is that shift of perspective. We can learn from everything if we so desire." - Biella Noble

When using awareness as the tool with which to deal with these psychologies, it's imperative to keep judgemental and critiquing emotions and feelings out of the equation.

At first glance this seems contradictory. Isn't the point and purpose of our awareness to *show* them how wrong they are? No, it's not. That would only demonstrate one doesn't fully understand the psychology of ego, superiority, hierarchy' and all of their subsections. We're not looking to play their game.

There may be certain circumstances when it would be appropriate to do so, but typically, it merely results in extra hassle, as the superiority needs to be constantly maintained. Tiresome. We instead aim to not deal with bullshitters at all and have them see there's no profit in dealing with us.

Pre-Emptive Prevention

"It takes graciousness, finesse, and nobility to efficiently and effectively deal with craziness. (ours)"

First, we can use awareness as a *pre-emptive* tool, as in: "I understand. I am able to recognise bullshit ego-hierarchy games, and thus they won't work on me and will be a waste of time, and likely will lead to exposure of such nonsense by anyone who tries such foolishness on me." We don't need to say this out loud, no need. If we're aware, it will exude from us.

For most BMNs, the risk of exposure isn't worth interaction when they perceive this awareness. Their ploys don't work on those who understand. To assert superiority over someone who isn't intimidated, who doesn't buy the BS, is next to impossible. As their only recourse then would be to use the *REAL* qualities and attributes of the individual for comparison.

A comparison the bullshitter doesn't want to get into, as the real truth about them isn't good. The reason they've taken to bullshit in the first place is to hide that awful truth about themselves. By showing we're aware of the full scope of their game, we demonstrate we're not a candidate for any kind of hierarchical comparison and interaction, an entanglement which only runs the risk of revealing the bullshitter's crappiness.

Neutral Awareness

"Bullshitters are finely attuned to vibe and implication. They fully get attitude and what's implied via awareness. They're animal-like in this. They respond not to words, but to energy, to intent, to emotional stability, and to the implications which flow from another's emotional state and awareness."

Coming to our remedy, we need to structure our awareness to show and reflect without judgement or critique. To show what *IS,* in a neutral way. A showing which is independent of our personal opinions. This isn't easy at first, as it's against our habit of sharing and communicating with personal opinion.

"One has to exercise extreme care when bursting the bubble of awareness which maintains the foolish notions of others."

Our objective is also to give the ego-mindset a view of what's happening, a view *THEY* also can use to adjust from. Once we fully understand this psychology, we know it's a chameleon psychology, taking on whatever is expedient to its goals and needs. Only if it can do so without loss of face. If the BMN ego can steal some usefulness without anyone knowing and pass it off as its own, this is the best, is desired, and gloated over.

If our awareness just shows what' is and leaves the interpretations to them, they can do with it what they will. Here it is using our awareness becomes powerful, because contained in that awareness of ours is the *possibility* of them seeing matters something like this: "Oh hell, I didn't realise I was maybe looking like a complete jerk and douche. I better not do that again. Makes me look terrible."

Since maintaining their status is so imperative to them, they don't want to risk "looking bad." It's important to understand, when that does happen, they stop caring, and throw out any pretence of niceness, becoming ugly and negative. An eventuality even more difficult to deal with. We thus leverage their fixation with appearances to positive ends.

"There's a necessity for: Appropriate-Intolerance."

We use sophistication to deal with bullshit and leave the individual themselves to correct according to their internal criteria as is most appropriate. In the greater scheme of things, this is how we learn and change. Internally, we have to come to a conclusion and see the sensibility or value by ourselves, then only is it truly our own.

We ever defy forced learning and change. We are, it seems, built by nature to resist programming. Understanding this also, we use our awareness in such a way that the information, the awareness, the understanding we communicate is a free sharing, to be used by others as they will. It's a reflection of what we perceive, absent of any valuations, moralising, judgements, opinions, etc.

Not a particularly easy practise when described in this way, but in reality it's actually not that difficult. We remove unwarranted emotion, especially self-pity, relying on our efforts to come to a comprehensive understanding, and thus empowering ourselves.

"When we trust, when we deliberately trust. When we trust, aware we're choosing to trust, when we do that, were being courageous. For courage is nothing but deliberate trust. That tiny little feeling we have of things not being quite right, or of disquiet, or ill-at-ease-ness, or discomfort of some kind, that's the feeling which comes from being courageous." - Biella Noble

Self-pity, feeling sorry for oneself, and being a "victim" is like a super-magnet to the bullshit psychology, exacerbating matters. (Perhaps it's nature's genius, providing a mechanism for aggravating a poor psychological choice, forcing us to not go down that path.)

We need an emotionally neutral awareness, a pure awareness, awareness of what is, of what we are, and of how we see things, an awareness of *understanding and discernment,* an awareness of k*nowing.*

Thus, in how we react and respond, we will benefit from applying the philosophy-of-opposite to ourselves, by not-doing what we abhor in others, even in small ways. Fully understanding not only the severity of the issue, of bullshit in society, and in our personal lives, but also understanding all of its ins and outs, its tricks and logics, enables us to deal with the problem.

"The task is to become comfortable with cock-eyedness because it's part of our lives, thus we have to make peace with our own silliness. The universe uses irrationality, illogicality, and insensibility to achieve goodness. It has to. Trust that cock-eyedness can lead to good."

Practical Positivity

"We can bypass the rabbit holes and subtle traps crafted by fools and bullshitters by just laughing at their ludicrous and wanton attention-seeking. We need to learn to purely laugh at the preposterous and the folly."

In the context of this book and this chapter, our remedy for dealing with bullshit and bullshitters lies in Awareness, Discernment, and Understanding. (AD U)

Also, there's remedy in dealing with bullshit in ways other than we typically do. Especially when it comes to the complicity of non-action and condoning via regarding bullshit as trivial. Once we understand, once we know how bullshit works and how bullshitters think, we have many options. Options which lead to remedy.

With the ability to recognise bullshit, we have the advantage of being able to set ourselves strategically, a massive advantage, which, along with our advantages of truth and realness, are advantages bullshit has no hope against.

"In the race for survival, predators can achieve impressive strengths and speeds—but research reveals that when it comes to strategy, their prey may have the

upper hand." - Scientific American

If we're to improve our lives, our everyday lives, and ourselves, we have to deal with the reality of bullshit. It's at the root of all trouble. When we look at any issue, no matter how serious, we see at its core, surrounding it and connected to it, the inevitable bullshit. This inescapable, but really serious truth seems to be somewhat overlooked. We see much which is wrong, yet fail to see the common cause of deceit, pretence, and disguise of flagrant negative intents and behaviours.

If we're to change, improve, and remedy what's wrong and bad, we have to change social consciousness of bullshit. Change to seeing it for the very real problem it is. We can't allow ourselves, individually and as a society, to be fooled and misdirected by the bullshit of bullshit. That's its trick, to make us think it's not really a problem, not a big deal, when in fact it is, and is the one common aspect of all problems and trouble.

Our task, each and every one of us, is to change social consciousness of this fact of the dangers and problems of deceit, to change how we individually perceive and relate to bullshit. No longer can we allow it, else we're complicit in spreading its disastrous consequences. We can't allow this.
We have to take a stand against deception, take action against all lying, and together, as a society, using awareness, discernment, and understanding, empower ourselves to call bullshit against bullshit!

"Essential questions to ask: Who says? Based on what? Why does it matter? What's the Intent here? How is this Appropriate?"

<<***>>

This ends: **The Psychology of Bullshit**

We sincerely hope you enjoyed and found value in this book, and if so, we kindly ask you to please leave us a review.
Reviews mean a tremendous amount to us, and we very much appreciate them. Thanks in advance. :)

Bonus material is found in the endnotes, as well as links to our ongoing discussion groups and projects.

Author Bios

Syl Sabastian's Bio:

"I admit to being an unusual person." - SS

From a comment on his profile pic, since writing one's own bio is so difficult:

"Beautiful and astounding. Kind of resembles an amazing character I know. Some call him the Weaver of the Unraveled, the Rekindler of Doused Fires, the Sandman of Endless Beaches, the Friend to the Friendless, the Harmonizer of Unsung Heroes. And some even call him Syl." - Na'Cher

From age 10, on the day he literally exploded a light-bulb, Syl Sabastian's acute life-long love affair with

Understanding began. Since then his focus on, and love of Awareness, or more accurately his struggle with non-awareness, has never let-up.

An intense reader in his youth, Syl absorbed over a book a day, including the classics read in chronological order, culminating in extensive science-fiction/fantasy/speculative reading. After transitioning to Applying and Living his philosophies, Appropriately, with Attunement the ever-present motivation and catalyst, it all morphed in time to an earnest propensity to write and communicate.

Syl and His Heart have owned restaurants, stores, online businesses, and travelled the world, while implementing and enjoying their life-perspectives of which he writes so deeply. As Biella is so fond of saying, "and there's More..."

"My life began, from earliest memory, with a peculiar precocious understanding of abstract concepts, a mystery which remains unexplained to any satisfaction. I feel I am traversing a circle back to my origin, except perhaps, now more aware of what I already knew." - From: The Young Man's Story

Syl is a great interview and an even better friend.

A Philosopher-Writer focusing on the Application of a comprehensive Practical-Personal-Philosophy. Creator of: The Philosophy of Appropriateness and: An A+ Philosophy. Writings range considerably, from extensive psychological perspectives to fiction. All connecting in one way or another to a unique vision. A consistent coherency permeates Syl Sabastian's extensive variety.

"Syl Sabastian is a Contemporary Philosopher and Writer, who exercises a glorious intellectual mind that's most admirable for its profundity and sharpness. Often

offering multiple sides of an argument, he provokes self-introspection. His aim is to uncover Appropriateness, Awareness, Attention, Application Attunement and more with a unique, high-level understanding of the profound intricacies that interlace these concepts." - TJT & PDJ, Owners of the Gateway Gazette, Entrepreneurs, Writers, Moms.

"*My blog is my best bio.*" -SS :) <3

"*You fascinate me, you really do. I think of myself as a big deep thinker... your writing, at least what I think I understand it to be about, sounds like the basis for either a belief-system or a wonderful self-help process. Am I anywhere near the mark? I think your writing, even about yourself, is amazing by the way. Quite poetic.*" - Andrew Reeves, Author, Screenwriter, Poet, Creator of The Empty World, The Voodoo Doll, Claire, The Dictionary of Stupid, and more.

Find Syl Sabastian on <u>Facebook</u> and Goodreads
And:
<u>www.sylsabastian.blogspot.com</u>
<u>www.nobelia.org</u>

*

And please don't forget to subscribe to the newsletter. :) :D <u>http://eepurl.com/drie4z</u>
Personal Consulting Services Available.

Elevia DeNobelia's Bio:

"I Feel like Alice in Wonderland; a perpetual explorer. My curiosity informs and instigates these articles, essays and books. I am inspired by Life and in turn try to pass on that inspiration and insight." - E DeN

Elevia's origins lie in simple but sublime beginnings. In the midst of what others would describe as trying circumstances, she made the most of her wonderful family life, developing a solid foundation of sturdy character. A focus she has spent her life extending and refining.

"A deeply loving woman who has been blessed to share her wisdom about the psychology of human behavior and the pitfalls to be aware of. The book demonstrates how she has preserved her true essence while understanding misguided patterns in others." - Angela R.N.

Ever the lover of knowledge and personal

development, Elevia set about engaging the world with the totality of her being. Everything she does, has done, has that component of developing and furthering her Awareness, Discernment and Understanding. Never afraid to embrace the unconventional in her personal quests and widespread travels, she has led a most different, adventurous, and ultimately, an exceedingly instructional life.

"Elevia has the articulation and wisdom of a wise sage. Listening to her thoughtful overview and advice on life and how we can master our harmful relationships and stick to our true path is a true gift..." - Jayne Ryan

From unusual relationships, living in a desert without electricity and running water and no close neighbours, having restaurants, one on top of a mountain, close interactions with a tribe of Bushmen, owning and running retail stores, to leaving it all behind to start over on a new continent with many attendant adventures too numerous to mention, Elevia's perpetual focus on learning and growth has served her well. Always everything to her was all under the umbrella focus of Self-Discovery and the Application of her continual learning. Each circumstance and situation adding volumes to her personal story and internal growth.

"Elevia is a soulful, questioning, and beautifully intelligent human being. She embraces, and shares her journey of humanity with a curious heart and a deep desire to know the deepest truth in any given situation." - Alba E Wejebe

She has a fierce passion and commitment to Sharing that which she feels is extremely impactful and important, especially were injustice and suffering are a factor. Particularly if it involves abuse and lack-of-awareness. She is passionately committed to spreading Goodness in the world, via Understanding and Awareness.

"A *different person, unique, strange and exotic. A child and a bold adult finding her way in the world.*" - Richard Neal

She *feels* the World, and through that intimate connection she communicates the depths of her Discernments, always striving to do so through the consuming artistry of her being, finding expression in everything she does, and is. As her friends frequently assert; being with Elevia is a joy, pleasure, and a gift, as she truly embodies and radiates all she believes and strives to apply.

"*Elevia is a brilliant and loving soul. She has so much to offer, I treasure spending time with her spirit and creativity.*" - Shari Silvey

"*Your thinking and expression is always so clearly defined, no weaving about,.... clear, concise, and to the point.*" - Sherry Ticktin

"*Very insightful with sensitivity to the many aspects of any subject.*" - Amy Winter

*

Endnotes

Why This Book?

What's the purpose of **The Psychology of Bullshit - Understanding the Bullshit-Manipulator-Narcissist? (BMN)** What does it wish to achieve?

This book aims to remove the environment bullshit and bullshitters need to exist. Let's look at the problem from the perspective of the issue of bullshit public figures who are abusers and who we've seen in the news.

They're outed, and that exposure, because they're well known and recognised, prevents them from continuing their bullshit and abuse. But what of the local unknown anonymous abuser? If they're outed locally they just move to where they're not known and can repeat the bullshit and abuse.

The solution lies not only in identifying the individuals specifically, but in being *able* to identify the *type* of person who does such things.

The goal of this book is to bring about a change of individual awareness and societal consciousness, awareness and understanding when it comes to recognising and knowing the bullshit mindset and psychology. In *all* its various degrees, not just the extreme versions.

That logic, those beliefs, that perspective of bullshit, all the way from the minor to the extreme, we can think of as only being able to exist in shadow. If, as a society, we now shine the light of awareness and understanding all around us, in our local communities, through our personal interactions, we eliminate those shadows, and the bullshit psychology and persona cannot exist any longer. This is the focus of our book. To bring about a change in social understanding.

We're aware, as a society, of the existence of such mindsets and psychologies, but because we don't fully understand, we fail to see them in our day-to-day lives. Especially when they're not yet extreme. But even when not extreme, they still do significant harm. A cancer. Like cancer, initially, in small bits, it's not noticeable, yet extremely consequential if not dealt with.

Our purpose is to bring about a societal evolution of consciousness when it comes to fully understanding what is involved with bullshit and how its seeming triviality or nuisance, or no-big-dealness, is exactly what fools us and lulls us into a false perspective. A perspective and belief which allows the cancer to fester and grow.

Once we realise, as a society, that making allowance, overlooking, looking away, denying, and our avoidance is exactly what leads to those extremes, and to all the pain, misery, and harm of all the in-between instances of bullshit, we can take responsibility and change, as a society.

We wish also with this book to leverage the compassion and goodness of good people. We don't want to give up on people who are lost in not-so-nice ways-of-being. We want to retain the hope there's some hope for them. It's exactly this the book wants to accomplish.

By removing the shadows of unawareness and lack of understanding, we create the opportunity to change for these lost persons. Simply through us making the effort to come to full understanding of what all is involved. Once we recognise and know, and see, and carry this awareness about with us, we exude that very light which brings about change and denies shadow.

So what does this mean in practical terms? Imagine yourself coming to a party here with us, in our home. At this party, other well-known people are also coming. People who aren't bullshitters, who're aware of bullshit, how it works, and understand how people work. People who're focused on goodness and love, but people at the same time who're totally honest, and who also don't tolerate bullshit. People for whom there's no place for bullshit in their lives, who see bullshit coming many miles away. People, whom the bullshitter can see know bullshit, are aware of bullshit, and understand all the doings of the bullshitter.

You come, bringing a bullshitter friend with you. How is this bullshitter likely to act in such an environment? Most likely they will behave differently. The climate just won't make it viable for them to bullshit. The option of bullshitting has been removed. Bullshit in such an environment would be lame, foolish, obvious, and utterly silly.

It's this climate, where bullshit is completely inappropriate, we wish to facilitate in society at large. This climate not only makes bullshit a childish option, but provides a climate of example for positive change in the bullshitter, as it's an honest climate, and if we're honest about goodness, how can we not also be positive?

Our book revolves around three key components: **Awareness, Discernment, and Understanding.** (AD U)

It's really tough to bring awareness, through in-depth discernment, to a topic which lacks understanding, especially when that topic isn't particularly positive. Hopefully we at least make this engagement interesting.

We need discernment to realise what we need to learn, but also, to discern what needs *UN-learning*. Our discernment leads us to becoming aware of what we need to know and what we don't want as part of our being. Knowing what we need and want isn't enough. To make learning our own, we have to truly understand, we have to make those knowings our own. Simply seeing knowledge, seeing it's value, isn't enough.

We have to understand to the point where we can explain the understanding as our own, then it becomes ours. In the context of this book, a thorough understanding of bullshit prevents us from indulging in bullshit. How can we do something when we're fully conscious of its wrongness, when we clearly and completely know the harm it will do? We can't. Fully understanding bullshit makes us not only better individuals, but better citizens of the world.

"Empathy has become a cheap word. Pretty much like 'love' has become a cheap word. 'Sorry,' too, another cheap word. However, there are people for whom love means love, sorry means truly being sorry, and empathy is something they can feel because they have the heart and mind and spirit to be able to put themselves in someone else's shoes. These are people who have character, ethics, integrity. These are the good people of the world. These are the unsung who actually make a real difference... whom our hearts salute!"

Gifts, Links & Bonuses

We hoped you enjoyed the results of our labours, and really hope you'll leave a Review.

Reviews are *huge* for authors, and make a tremendous difference when it comes to getting others involved. We hope you'll contribute to spreading the awarenesses contained in the book by leaving your review. Feel free to leave a review even if you've only partially read the book, doesn't matter.

Please visit our website, Nobelia.org. Here you can not only access loads of content, but also stay connected and up to date with what's happening in our world. We have much going on, not only connected to this book, and the topics it touches, but in many other fields and topics.

We would love you to connect with us in the various ways possible. Subscribe to our Mailing List and join our Discussion Group: Self-Awareness Self-Improvement (SaSi) Discussion Group where much free and bonus material is available. We mail out new content automatically, as well as any news and announcements concerning other relevant projects and future books. (Coming soon, another book of The Realism Series.)

We have constantly ongoing discussions connecting to all of our topics, themes and projects, all connecting back to Self-Awareness, Self-Improvement, and Self-Discovery in some way. Please join in or simply observe as many like to do. All good. :) <3

<<<◇>>>

Made in the USA
Thornton, CO
01/01/25 13:29:20

6c5ef53c-df17-4a6c-ab8a-4f649ee0772cR01